COMMERCE AND CULTURE

FROM PRE-INDUSTRIAL ART TO POST-INDUSTRIAL VALUE

. . . why don't we discard the word 'art' and replace it with the word 'work'?

Milton Glaser , 1989

CONTENTS

Written and Edited by Stephen Bayley

Researched by Saskia Partington

Designed by David Davies Associates

Printed and Bound in Great Britain

by Penshurst Press Ltd

Typeset by Wells Photoset

ISBN No: 1 872005 004

FOREWORD

The creation of any museum is unusual; the creation of a Design Museum even more so. Since they betray contemporary preoccupations, a history of the national temperament could be written in terms of the museum. You have classical archaeology in the age of the 'grand tour', ethnography as explorers pushed into darker continents, science in the century of mechanised war and now, approaching a millenium...design.

There are cynics who interpret the recent fascination with design as simply another evanescent management fad, rather as work-study engineering in the twenties or personnel in the fifties were also presented as means of reviving flagging industries. But design is not only about business, as the Design Museum intends to show by opening out the study of design away from objects as ends in themselves and into the world of ideas. The heritage of design is at least as interesting as literature or the fine arts, its future perhaps even more promising.

Commerce and Culture sets the agenda for the Design Museum, by looking at those ideas − about tradition, reproduction, value and meaning − which influence our interpretation of the things we see, buy and use. Its starting point is a conventional one. Most of us were educated to believe that commerce is something distinct from culture, but it is the purpose of this exhibition to suggest that it is in fact a part of it. The stigmatisation of commerce and the consequent separation of art from industry is historically specific − a consequence of the social and technical upheavals brought about by mass production − and would have been unintelligible to artists and patrons of the past. Once, commerce and culture were all one. In the future it looks as though they will be one again. This startling assertion was stimulated by the curious observation that the gap between shops and museums is closing. Shops are becoming more 'cultural', as anybody who has been to Ralph Lauren's Madison Avenue store can testify. Here you find merchandise for sale side-by-side with a permanent exhibition about values and style, set in an environment somewhat reminiscent of the Frick.

Meanwhile, a few blocks away in the Metropolitan Museum, the first thing you hear when you cross the threshold is the whirr of cash-registers, evidence of a mighty commercial machine running at considerable speed. Shops and museums have a great deal in common. Urban, predominantly middle class, dedicated to exhibition, committed to consumption, either of images, ideas or goods. Once separated only by the availability of their contents (for sale in the stores, only for display in the museums), new attitudes and new technologies tend to erode this distinction between merchandise and collections. The first *museion* was the home of the Muses, Erato, Terpsichore and Clio among them. These nine children of Zeus and Mnemosyne, at first only daughters of memory, became identified with the arts and sciences. They have now been joined by industry, technology and commerce. The Design Museum is their home. There are those who will say that it is absurd to venerate sometimes banal objects in a Museum, but it is not the purpose of the Design Museum to add specious value to the commonplace by putting it on a plinth. Rather, the purpose is to provide a frame-work of ideas to explain the everyday.

The graphic designer, Milton Glaser, wants to replace the word 'art' with the word 'work'. This is what will happen when commerce and culture elide. In more senses than one, this exhibition is just a beginning.

Stephen Bayley April, 1989.

SPACE PEN Approved by NASA for use in outer space. Writes at any angle without stopping, on glossy photographs, over grease, under water. Unconditionally guaranteed. Classic styling. Detachable cap. Positive pressurised ink feed.
90mm
Gold Pen M71594
Silver Pen M73606
Black Pen M88590
Black/Gold Pen M70584
Black/Silver Pen M83615
£7.99

SURVIVAL TOOL Solid stainless steel multi-tool comprising pliers, crimps, wire cutters, file, bottle opener, can opener, scraper, 6, 7, 8mm and crosshead screwdrivers, 20cm ruler. Contained in black carry pouch.
Folds to 112mm × 23mm × 12mm
Survival Tool M78571
£15.99

PICNIC CAPSULE Canister contains four plates, four tumblers, four spoons, four forks, one knife, one bottle/can opener. Stainless steel cutlery. Shoulder strap.
290mm × 110mm
Black Capsule M80609
£39.99

MINI MAGLIGHT Pocket flashlight precision engineered to demanding specifications. Type used by the New York Police Force. Adjustable focus beam, table lamp function. Water resistant. Spare bulb supplied. Requires two AA batteries.
Length 145mm
Black Maglite M78607
Grey Maglite M80572
Blue Maglite M87579
Silver Maglite M81602
£19.99

2

2, 4. The idea of the *catalogue*, whether it describes a collection of art or a selection of, merchandise, is shared by museums and stores.

When the first Next *Directory* appeared in 1988 (top and bottom), its sophistication closed the gap between a shopping guide and a reference book.

3. Antoine Watteau's celebrated masterpiece, *L'Enseigne de Gersaint* (1721), was created not as a work of art to hang in a museum, but as a shopkeeper's sign.

3

4

WATTEAU,
ART AND TRADE

As the twentieth century ends, commerce and culture are coming closer together. The distinction between life and art has been eroded by fifty years of enhanced communications, ever-improving reproduction technologies and increasing wealth. This has changed patterns of behaviour, as well as the character of institutions. Shopping has been described as one of the legitimate cultural pursuits of the 1980s,[1] while at the same time, traditional museums are realising the hidden value of their collections, treating them not merely as cabinets of curios, nor even as a scholarly resource, but ever more frequently as assets which can be reproduced, merchandised and marketed. Knowledge is valuable and both shops and museums are realising it. Shops by adding quality of experience to the banal exchange of goods for money; museums by selling information and maybe, one day, even selling objects too...

1   By Lord Gowrie, Chairman of Sotheby's, in an address at the London Business School, 1988. Sotheby's is owned by Alfred Taubman, whose fortune derives from retail property development.

This new synthesis blurs the edges of our value system, outraging both the critical left (which interprets the process of elision as the Muses whoring in the market-place) and the conservative right (which condemns the same process as vulgar populism). But no-one denies the change is taking place. Withal, it is possible to speculate that maybe in future museums and shops will become the same institution, huge repositories of objects, images and information – in anticipation, they have been christened 'knowledge centres' – with everything available for inspection, comparison and for sale.

The appetite for knowledge is both a symptom and a cause of this potentially huge change. The public is becoming better educated and consequently more discriminating, demanding superior merchandise and better environments from shops and at the same time expecting museums and galleries to provide a service which is not simply scholarly *de haut en bas*, but treats them more as clients in the information and entertainment business.

A similar process is at work in publishing and television: in certain magazines it is actually difficult to distinguish editorial content from paid advertising insertions. Occasionally, this is deliberate, as in the case of the 'magalogs' published by leading stores, including Harrods in Britain and Bloomingdale's in the United States. When the chain store Next published its *Directory* in 1988, suddenly a mail order catalogue began to look somewhat like an international design guide. On television, the advertisements are often 'the best things on tv'[2] with larger budgets than the programmes they punctuate as commercial breaks: thirty seconds of Coke or Colgate often has superior production values to thirty minutes of Hollywood fizz or soap.

2   The expression is Jonathan Price's. His book of that title was published in New York in 1979.

This historical moment is one of very specific character, but does it mean – with shops becoming more educational and museums becoming more sensitive to the market-place – that civilisation is under threat, that the values so carefully nurtured by a discriminating elite are menaced by the barbarous populism, born of politically inspired consumerism?

The jeopardy is only real if you accept the Romantic model of the world, an idea crafted during the early years of the nineteenth century, in defence against industrial production and mass-consumption which looked about to undermine the tastes of a powerful elite. Artists took refuge in styles of behaviour and expression which validated their work by its *distance* from the public and consumerism.

But art was not always as remote from the everyday as the Romantic artist longed for it to be, nor was it as inaccessible as it was in the traditional museum. In fact, it is a curious paradox that, while not immediately obvious, it was the first museums which contributed to the banalisation of art. As André Malraux observed, art galleries "turned gods into statues."[3] While once, a Greek votive sculpture, a Romanesque crucifix or a Renaissance Madonna were magical, mystical, religious images, by the time they were assembled into public museums, as the voracious Western appetite for consumption demanded, they were demoted from deities to mere statues and pictures. The museum arose out of the same social, cultural, historical conditions of the nineteenth century as the department store and other institutions such as hospitals and prisons. Each has imposed on the spectator a wholly new attitude to the appreciation of artefacts...whether works of art or consumer durables. Civilisation is not really under threat from these changes. On the contrary, the synthesis of commerce and culture is a unifying process, bringing together the two appetites for consumption of knowledge and of goods which were once artificially separated.

Perhaps the most perfect example of art and its relation to trade is Antoine Watteau's exquisite painting, *L'Enseigne de Gersaint*.[4] Watteau (1684-1721) was a painter of languor and grandeur, of poetic scenes from the Commedia dell'arte; his are pictures which offer vignettes of a theatre of courtly conversations. On election to the Academie Française he was described as a 'peintre de fêtes galantes', a category all his own. But throughout his brief career, he became increasingly sensitive to the commercial opportunities of a new age, particularly after a visit to England in 1719, where, according, to the Goncourts:

> "Watteau began to acquire a taste for money of which he had hitherto made light, despising it to the point of indifference."[5]

On his return to Paris he lodged with the dealer, Edmé Gersaint, who kept a shop called Au Grand Monarque on the Pont Notre-Dame. Gersaint recalled that

> "Watteau...asked me if I would allow him, in order to keep his fingers supple...to paint a sign to be exhibited outside his shop. I was not in favour of the idea because I would have preferred him to work on something more substantial; but seeing that it would give him pleasure, I consented...This was the only work in which he ever took the slightest pride."[6]

It is sobering for those who believe that great pictures belong only in museums to learn that one of the most celebrated eighteenth-century works of art, painted by one of the great poets of the century, was, in fact, created as a fascia board for a Paris shop...even if it did remain there for only fourteen days before another enterprising dealer snapped it up.

For the Romantics, the tragic, itinerant Watteau was a prototype hero. This passed through to some of the fashion magazines of the nineteenth century which encouraged their readers to affect Watteau gestures both in their clothes and their interiors. This outraged the Goncourts, who, in order to salvage art from the depredations of middle class *use*, turned Watteau into a genius, just as history turned his fascia board into a work of art.

Commerce and Culture is concerned with middle-class use, about how consumer choice can effectively be made against a background of fast changing social, technical and artistic values. The inversion of standards so clearly illustrated by *L'Enseigne de*

3   See Essay #2.

4   Now in the Charlottenburg Palace, Berlin.

5   Edmond and Jules de Goncourt *French Eighteenth-Century Painters*, 1948.

6   Edmé Gersaint in *Catalogue de la collection du feu M. Quentin de Lorangere*, 1744. Translated by Anita Brookner in *Watteau*, 1967.

Gersaint, where a fine artist willingly put himself in the service of 'trade' are as familiar in our own century, but no better understood.

The Victoria and Albert Museum now has a subsidiary called 'V&A Enterprises'. One recent venture has been a collaboration with the Habitat home furnishings stores. Habitat is using the Museum's textile collections, including designs by C. H. Townsend and C. F. A. Voysey, as source material for a new consumer range called the 'Habitat/V&A Collection'.

In turn, Habitat sponsored an exhibition called *The Textiles of the Arts and Crafts Movement*. Previously the chain store Laura Ashley launched its 'Bloomsbury Collection', using designs by Vanessa Bell and Duncan Grant first seen at the Sussex farmhouse, Charleston. Similarly, perhaps the single most exciting thing to happen in the torpid world of British furniture during 1988 was the decision by the Lutyens family to begin reproducing designs made by Sir Edwin for the Viceroy's Palace in New Delhi (1920-31).

Appropriately, it was exhibitions which inspired Laura Ashley's decision to recreate the arts and crafts of the rural Bloomsbury set for their customers of the late eighties. It was after seeing the Arts Council's exhibition *The Thirties* (1979) and the Crafts Council's *Omega Workshop* (1984) show which gave the company's design director, Nick Ashley, the idea. Interestingly, Duncan Grant himself would probably have approved. In his own lifetime he had designs for dinner and tea services put into production by Wilkinson and Brain, but the market potential was never realised since distribution and communication during the thirties was considerably more primitive than it is today. Grant explained his own predicament:

> "If there existed today some form of liaison between art and industry, some centre to which artists could offer their work and on which manufacturers could draw for ideas, the cost to industry would be no higher than that of the individual employment of working 'designers'...Indeed, as things are, the idea that an independent artist demands a prohibitive fee is quite unfounded."[7]

7 *Industrial Arts*, Autumn 1936.

While Habitat and Laura Ashley are offering their customers the stuff that was once in museums, even supermarkets want to add the allure of culture to their perishable merchandise. A press advertisement for Sainsbury's shows Gainsborough's painting *Mr and Mrs Joseph Andrews* (c.1750) made out of cooking chocolate, while other ads in the same series use extraordinary copy-writing whose purpose is surely more subtle and complex than merely trying to stimulate sales of comestibles. Once all that was required to sell sherry was a luscious packshot of the bottle, nowadays Sainsbury's sell it with an authoritative, even educational text, somewhere in style between the oenology of Hugh Johnson and the travelogue of Norman Lewis. Here is copy-writer Richard Foster on the humble manzanilla:

> "About 20km north-west of Jerez lies the small fishing village of Sanlucar de Barraneda...Sanlucar's coastal position gives it a cooler, more humid climate than that of Jerez...Ideal conditions...for the development of 'Flor', a film of yeast that forms naturally on the surface of sherry in the cask."[8]

8 This campaign was current in Britain during 1988.

That ads for sherry nowadays read like text books, that Panasonic use Cubist pictures to sell office machines and Mercedes-Benz is pleased to compare itself to the eighteenth-century visionary architect, Claude-Nicolas Ledoux, are symptoms of an age demanding *value* and *meaning*, even in very ordinary, everyday things. In product design, functional excellence is now the baseline and to be successful consumer goods have to offer something more culturally seductive than mere efficiency. Customers demand what the advertisers call *shared values*: when Renault introduced a new

There's no great secret to making great chocolate. It's all a question of cocoa solids.

The more you put in (powder and butter) the richer and tastier the chocolate.

No other cooking chocolate contains more

Sainsbury's cooking chocolate. It's not a chocolate fake.

cocoa solids than Sainsbury's De Luxe, which weighs in with 51%. (Some chocolate-flavoured cake toppings contain as little as 12%.)

To put our chocolate's cooking properties to the test we gave Britain's most creative cake-makers an open brief.

As you can see they, and Sainsbury's Deluxe, met the challenge.

Putting the rich chocolate taste to the test, however, is a far simpler and equally rewarding undertaking.

Good food costs less at Sainsbury's.

5

From the unique creation of the Hammam Baths, to the fragrant allure of Penhaligon's Hammam Bouquet.

OUT OF FIERY MISTS

The origins of the Turkish Bath lie buried in the mists of time. An idea conceived by the Romans and then adopted **A Shroud of Time** by the East, who christened it *Hammam*, meaning steam-bath.

England indulged in the Turkish delight and by 1250, London was overflowing with baths, or 'stews' as they were known. By 1850, the medical profession had gained an appetite for them and prescribed the heat treatment for almost every ailment. **Penhaligon's Perfume.** Some people ventured into baths whilst under the spell of writers and poets, who had captured the joys of Eastern bathing in their work. Unfortunately, these literary descriptions did not reflect British baths, which were merely watered down versions of genuine *Hammams*.

Then in 1862, the Hammam Baths opened their Eastern doors to Western gentlemen **Hammam Baths.** at 76 Jermyn Street, St. James, London. There servants (*Cahgis*), would pour coffee from filigree pots into china cups and presented guests with gifts of sweetmeats, Oriental sherbet, seasonal fruits and uncut Persian tobacco. Plants and flowers sweetly-scented the air and the overall impression was one of the greatest luxury.

After a period of repose, the bather then donned a loin-cloth (*maksam*) and shoulder-towel (*futa*). An attendant then led him to the hot-room (*hararah*), where he lay like a sacrificial offering until he began to show a gentle flow of perspiration. It was at this moment that the bathman (*tellak*), performed the massage

ritual and with a camel-hair glove, swept the body from the neck to the heels.

Should the bather have desired hotter climates, he visited another two rooms before passing into the spa-chamber. Inside, a needle-shower would hiss and douse him down. Afterwards he would walk into the washing room (*hanafeyeh*), where a tellak prepared a lather of soft water and soap in large copper bowls. A wheel-shaped brush fashioned from the fibres of palm trees, was used to 'shampoo' the body. Water was drawn in leather pitchers from marble basins and poured over the bather's frame.

The next step was to take the plunge and jump into the cold pool. After the fiery mists, the icy waters were a shock to the system. Finally, the bather was vigourously rubbed down and wrapped in warm robes. With a body as sleek as satin and shining like alabaster, he was conducted back to the *mushlakh*. There he was fanned with ostrich feathers and fed with Eastern delicacies.

To complete the invigorating experience, bathers would call upon the shaving services of Mr. William Henry Penhaligon. His shop being conveniently placed next door to the baths. Although a barber by trade, Mr. Penhaligon made a name for himself as 'a creator of exquisite and unique scents'. Indeed, they won him worldwide renown and popularity. They even gained the approval of Royalty.

A favourite fragrance and a natural choice of the gentlemen bathers was Hammam Bouquet.

AND ROSY SHADOWS...

It's concoction required meticulous skill. Just as Mr. Penhaligon took the name from the **Hammam Bouquet.** Turkish Baths, he extracted the oil of Otto from the Turkish Rose.

He blended it with oils drawn from English Lavender and Jasmin. A hint of Sandalwood provided the finishing touch.

Sadly, the barber's shop and Baths of Jermyn Street remain only as memories of a bygone age. However, the Penhaligon spirit and scents linger on at 41, Wellington Street, in London's Covent Garden and at our other premises in Mayfair, the Burlington Arcade and the City.

These include a soothing aftershave balm, an invigorating shampoo, luxurious bath oil, scented soaps and of course the renowned

Hammam Bouquet Extract. There are also a host of other fragrances hanging in the balmy air.

To create them, we always go by the book, which happens to be the very same one that Mr. Penhaligon used for recording all his formulas. In these days of change, it's heartening to know that not everything disappears in the mists of time.

PENHALIGON'S
Perfumers, Established 1870

6

5. As commerce and culture elide, advertisements change character, assuming an instructive, almost educational role. Abbott Mead Vickers use Gainsborough to sell Sainsbury's chocolate.

6. As an advertisement for Penhaligon's, WCRS did not create an injunction to *buy*, but wrote a magazine feature.

7. Habitat sponsored a textile exhibition at the Victoria and Albert Museum and in return acquired the rights to reproduce Arts and Crafts designs.

8. While shops become more conscious of culture and tradition, museums become more commercially aware. New York's Museum of Modern Art has a shop which lives off its collections.

9. Andy Warhol's ironic celebration of tinned soup came full circle when in 1985, Campbell's commissioned a painting to celebrate the launch of a new food product.

model to the American market in 1988, they used the actor George C. Scott to present the car, since market research had shown that Scott, best known for his role as General Patton, represented strength, dependability and honesty. These were exactly the values Renault wanted to share. To a social theorist of the left, such as W. F. Haug, these charades demonstrate the vapidity of high consumption capitalism. Design appears as just another way of stimulating sales, no different in substance from hiring an actor to hype your new car.

But if design and art are becoming subsidiary to sales, the consumer is bright enough to realise it. Decades of emphasis on surface and packaging have taught that mere possession of goods is not enough, especially when the Japanese have proven that anything can be made ever more efficiently at ever reduced cost, thus making any notion of intrinsic value in hardware mere sentiment. The make-up of the new consumer, hardened by functional perfection in the goods he buys, changes the purpose of shopping and of museums. An executive at the advertising agency, Ogilvy & Mather, defined the new consumer:

> "In the 1960s and 1970s, possession alone were sufficient. But nowadays the concept of ideal homes stuffed with material goods doesn't work. Now that most people have a full pantry of electronic wonders, people are working for meaning beyond the fact of possessions. Possessing is not enough."[9]

9 *Financial Times*, 26th September 1987.

In commercial response, advertising no longer merely offers merchandise, but suggests experience. The most successful television ads of recent years have been Bartle Bogle Hegarty's beautifully crafted campaigns for Levi's jeans and Audi's cars. These do not make an offer for sale, but rather seek to provide *ambience* and layers of imagery for the consumer to decode. In them texture is at least as important as message. Buy me and become me, they seem to be saying.

If the cultural response is presently more difficult to define, there is evidence everywhere easy to detect. In the early sixties Andy Warhol, who was an advertising art director, began his career as a painter with his ironic canvases depicting deadpans and dayglo tins of Campbell's Soups. By 1985, with endorsements for Pontiac, Diet Coke and Vidal Sassoon already in his portfolio, and a print or canvas in every Modern Art museum, Warhol's avant-gardism had been comfortably accommodated into the mainstream of both commerce and culture. In that year Campbell's commissioned Warhol to *paint* its latest product, a dried soup. Unveiled at New York's Whitney Museum, this event served also as the product launch as well as a *vernissage*.

Between Watteau on the Pont Notre-Dame and Warhol on Madison Avenue there are two hundred and fifty years where commerce and culture have been involved and then separated and then involved again. Out of this anthology of conflicts and liaisons emerge the special circumstances of the late twentieth century. To some, the disturbance of the existing order and the promiscuous adaptation of art in the service of business is only evidence of a corruption in standards and a decadence characteristic of the *fin-de-siècle*. But what the future holds is not a narrowing of choice in a market full of lowest common denominators, but an expansion of it in pursuit of highest common factors. Watteau is no less an artist for having painted a fascia board while Sainsbury's is no less effective a business for producing advertisements which entertain and educate instead of condescending and exploiting.

For the consumer, whether in a shop or in a museum, commerce and culture, being more than the simple sum of their parts, offer an enriching experience.

MUSEUMS WITHOUT WALLS

André Malraux

Malraux (1901-76) published his first book, a collection of prose poems, in 1921. As a novelist, he won the Prix Goncourt in 1924, but he became increasingly interested in the visual arts. His *Psychology of Art* (begun in 1939) and later *Museum Without Walls*, brought new subtlety and sophistication to popular art books. Malraux was fascinated by the paradoxical idea that, while the traditional museum tended to rob paintings and sculpture of their original religious value, modern communications allowed everyone to enjoy art more easily.

So vital is the part played by the great art museums in our approach to works of art today that it is hard for us to realise that no museums exist, none has ever existed, in lands where the civilization of modern Europe is, or was, known; and that, even among us, they have existed for less than a couple of centuries. They bulked so large in the nineteenth century and are so much a part of our lives today that we forgot they have imposed on the spectator a wholly new attitude towards the work of art.

A Romanesque crucifix was not conceived as a work of sculpture; nor Duccio's Madonna as a picture. Even Phidias's 'Pallas Athene' was not primarily a statue.

The reason why historical painting subsequently played so great a part is that the plastic arts (until the invention of photography and, later, of the cinema) were in a high degree arts of the imagination. An unreal world of history, fantasy and the sublime was quite as much the painter's province as the writer's.

Italy, when not creating imaginary figures, practised an imaginative portrayal of real people. For an Italian the whole duty of the artist was to translate things seen into an imagined world of beauty; to include them in that glowing panorama of high art which spanned three full centuries. Though a beautiful body painted by an artist was not bound to be a beautiful painting, a beautiful painting (other than a portrait) was necessarily, for the Italians, one of a beautiful body. And once the ideas of art and beauty had parted company, Italian painting fell into a decline. Thus, after having served for the creation of a supernal world, plastic art was chiefly, over many centuries, the means of creating an imagined or transfigured world.

And then the Art Museum brought about a drastic change, transforming the artist's visions into pictures, as it transformed the gods into statues. Even the portrait became, primarily, a work by such and such an artist. Though Caesar's bust and the equestrian Charles V remain for us Caesar and Charles V, Duke Olivares has become pure Velasquez. What do we care who that Helmeted Man *or the* Man with the Glove *may have been in real life? For us their names are Rembrandt and Titian. The men who sat for them have lapsed into nonentity. Until the nineteenth century a work of art was essentially a representation of something real or imaginary, which preceded and conditioned its existence as a work of art. Only in the artist's eyes was painting specifically painting, and often, even for him, it chiefly meant a poetic or dramatized presentation of his subject. The effect of the Art Museum was to suppress the model in almost every portrait. Divesting the works it brought together of their functions, it did away with the significance of Saint and Saviour; ruled out associations of sanctity,*

11. Works of religous art, whether votive sculptures or a Romanesque cross, once had a functional, magic purpose which is denied in a museum.

11

13

12

12 – 14. Although some museums including the Louve, Paris (above and top right, bottom right), have earlier origins, in essence they are all responses to industrialisation, which distanced art from life and put it into institutions. Seen here: the Nike of Samothrake on the Escalier Daru and the Consistory Door from Toulouse.

14

qualities of adornment and possession, of likeness or imagination. In the Art Museum each exhibit is taken to mean something different from itself this specific difference being its raison d'etre *and the justification for its presence there. In the past a Gothic statue was an integral part of the Cathedral, a classical picture was tied up with the setting of its period; a work of art, in short, had always been closely connected with its surroundings, and was never expected to consort with works of different mood and outlook. For otherwise, it was kept apart from them, to be the more appreciated by the spectator. But the art gallery, having removed it from its place of origin, juxtaposes it to rival or even hostile works. Every art collection is an anthology of contrasts.*

The reason why not until quite recently, and only under European influence, Asia has had experience of the art collection is that for an Asiatic, artistic contemplation and the picture gallery are incompatible. In China the full enjoyment of works of art necessarily involves ownership, except where religious art is concerned; above all, it requires their isolation. A painting is not exhibited, but unfurled before an art lover who is in a proper state of grace; its function for fifteen centuries has been to deepen and adorn his communion with the universe. The practice of pitting works of art against each other, an intellectual activity, is the opposite pole from the mood of mental relaxation which alone makes contemplation possible. To the Asiatic's thinking an art collection is as preposterous as would be a concert in which the audience had to listen to an ill-assorted miscellany of pieces performed without a break.

Indeed it is undeniable that for over a century our commerce with art has been growing more and more intellectualized. The art gallery invites criticism of each of the impressions, and expressions, of the world it brings together; and a query as to what brought them together. To the 'delight of the eye' there has been added – owing to the sequence of styles and seemingly antagonistic schools – an awareness of art's heroic quest, and its long struggle to remould the sorry scheme of things. Indeed, an art gallery is one of the places which show Man at his noblest. But, while segregating works from their birthplace and natural setting, it has not isolated them from history. Our knowledge is more comprehensive than our museums, and ranges further afield. The visitor to the Louvre knows he will not find significantly represented there the great English artists, or Goya, or Michelangelo, or Piero della Francesca. Inevitably, in a place where the work of art has no longer any function other than that of being a work of art, and at a time when the artistic exploration of the world is in active progress, the assemblage of so many masterpieces – from which, nevertheless, so many more are missing – conjures up in the mind's eye all the world's masterpieces. How indeed could this truncated possible fail to evoke the whole gamut of the possible?

Of what is it necessarily deprived? Of all that forms an integral part of a whole (stained-glass, frescos); of all that cannot be moved; of objects such as sets of tapestry which are difficult to display; and, chiefly, of all that the collection is unable to acquire. Even when the greatest zeal has gone to its making, a collection owes much to happy opportunity. All Napoleon's victories did not enable him to bring the Sistine to the Louvre, and no art-patron, however wealthy, will take to the Metropolitan Museum the Royal Portal of Chartres or the Arezzo frescos. From the eighteenth to the twentieth century what migrated was the portable; many more pictures by Rembrandt than Giotto frescos have found their way to dealers' shops and auction-rooms. Thus the Art Museum, born when the easel-picture was the one living form of art, came to be a pageant not of colour but of pictures.

The 'grand art tour' rounded it off in the nineteenth century. But in those days a man who had seen the totality of European masterpieces was a very rare exception. Gautier saw Italy only when he was thirty-nine; Edmond de Goncourt when he was thirty-three, Hugo only as a small boy; Baudelaire and Verlaine, never. The same holds good for

Spain; for Holland rather less, as Flanders was relatively well known.
The eager crowds that thronged the Salons – a public largely composed of real
connoisseurs – owed their art education to the Louvre. Baudelaire never set eyes on the
masterworks of El Greco, Michelangelo, Masaccio, Piero della Francesca or Grünewald.

What had he seen? What had Stendhal seen? What (until 1900) had been seen by
all those writers whose views on art still impress us as revealing and significant; whom
we take to be speaking of the same works as those we know, and referring to the same
data as those available to us? They had visited some galleries, and seen reproductions
of a handful of the masterpieces of European art; most of their readers had seen even
less. In the art knowledge of those days there was an hiatus, a pale of ambiguity, due to
the fact that the comparison of a picture in the Louvre with another in Madrid was that
of a present picture with a memory. Though engravings may be there to help, the visual
memory is far from infallible, and weeks lay between their personal inspections of the
two canvases. This handicap of the nineteenth-century art lover was much like ours
regarding stained-glass windows.

Nowadays an art student can consult colour reproductions of most of the world's great
pictures. Hitherto the connoisseur duly visited the Louvre and minor galleries and
memorized what he saw, as best he could. But there were many more significant works
in the Louvre than even the best trained, most retentive mind could register. Whereas the
modern connoisseur has far more great works accessible to his eyes than those contained
in even the greatest of museums. For an Imaginary Art Museum without precedent has
come into being, and it will carry infinitely further that process of 'intellectualization'
which began with the comparison, partial and precarious though it had to be, of the
originals in the galleries and museums of the Western world.

THE VALUE OF TRADITION

With commerce and culture feeding off each other, how are standards to be judged?

The idea of tradition is fundamental to Western civilization, although it is sometimes honoured as much in the breach as the observation. A great deal of conventional art history is concerned with establishing the course of the classical *tradition*, of looking at the way in which the artistic, philosophical and architectural cultures of Greece and Rome have been passed down and occasionally distorted on their way to successive European civilisations, including ours.

Until the Modern Movement of the 1920s attempted a definitive break with tradition, there had been more than two thousand years of continuous renewal and imitation of classical forms in architecture and sculpture. Important studies, including Jean Seznec's *La Survivance des Dieux Antiques* (1940) and Erwin Panofsky's *Renaissance and Renascences in Western Art* (1960), showed that the Renaissance of fourteenth-century Italy was not an isolated eruption of refreshed classical learning, but more simply one particularly impressive example of it.

What distinguished the Italian Renaissance from its medieval forebears was its self-consciousness, its sophisticated awareness of historical distance. While a sense of continuity, or at least of timely repair, was inherent in, say, the Holy Roman Empire, the Renaissance of Ficino, Medici, Raphael and Brunelleschi was more essentially modern in its appreciation of the past and in its wishing to sample and be inspired by the very best of it.

Why this is relevant to the study of design five centuries later is another question of awareness, this time our own. Now that the definitive break attempted by the Modern Movement can be seen for what it was − a heroic initiative, but a historically specific and a creatively limited one − there is much speculation about another 'classical revival' and the suggestion accompanies it that superior values attach to this anticipated revival, values which were denied throughout most of this century.[1]

[1] See Essay #4

The present circumstances are made more complex by two novel factors, unknown in the Renaissance: communications and manufacturing technology. The entire history of civilization is available for our consumption and new technologies allow anything from the past (whether, say, an architectural detail or a work of art) to be reproduced with perfect fidelity. But surely our historical distance from the Renaissance, let alone the Classical past which it revived, is so isolating that a modern 'classical rival' would not truly be a part of an established tradition of renewal and imitation, but rather mere piracy. Surely what we are being offered is plagiarism and pastiche, not an authentic expression of culture and if this happens today in architecture, then it will happen tomorrow in design, but for the moment it is architecture which provides the most revealing clues to the solution of this contemporary conundrum.

The idea of a *canon* in architecture was established during the Renaissance, but it was a fragile thing, depending on the Roman architect Vitruvius' single book, *De Architectura* and a handful of surviving buildings. Vitruvius established the Doric, Ionic and Corinthian orders of architecture to which were later added the Tuscan and the Composite. By time Palladio published his *Quattro Libri dell'Architettura* in Venice (1570), the process of canonisation was complete, a language was established

15, 16. Classical architecture depends on a canon of designs, passed on through literature, including Vitruvius (Italian ed. 1521) and Henry Wotton (1624).

THE PREFACE.

Our principall Master is Vitruuius and so I shall often call him; who had this felicitie, that he wrote when the Roman Empire was neere the pitch; Or at least, when Augustus (who favoured his endeauours) had some meaning (if he were not mistaken) to bound the Monarchie: This I say was his good happe; For in growing and enlarging times, Artes are commonly drowned in Action: But on the other side, it was in truth an vnhappinesse, to expresse himselfe so ill, especially writing (as he did)

16

17

17. Canaletto's *Feast Day of S Roch* (1735) shows the authentic tradition of Venetian townscape.

18

19

18, 19. Classicism provides a language of design which is flexible, but limited, Palladio's designs, from the *Quattro Libri* (1570) are capable of many variations. Palladio's Villa Rotonda, Vicenza (1550s; left) and Burlington's Chiswick House, London (1725; right).

20. Quinlan Terry's Richmond Riverside was built in 1988. A masterly deceit, it disguises a speculative office development, denying the structural logic of classicism.

20

which admitted a range of expression, but only within a restricted vocabulary. Attempts by French architects including Charles Perrault, actually to add nationalistic novelties to the canon were short-lived. Certainly, if confidence is a result of maturity, Palladio's own buildings seem evidence enough of a well established language which is easy to acquire, but capable of immense force and subtlety of expression.

But after the cultural schism of the Modern Movement, to say nothing of the technical changes entailed by telecommunications, jet travel, fast-track construction, synthetic materials, computing, diesel engines, pluralism and system building, and everything else which makes the assumptions of Greece and Rome and even Venice look rather homespun, can an architecture based on classical tradition, using the once sublime language of the orders, be anything more than mere copying? This is a question which effects much more than just the history of building, for if architects are content to recycle established forms and details, why should not designers of, say kitchen machines or cars, also merely work within the limited repertoire of what is known to be acceptable?

The very idea of 'classicism', at least so called, dates only from the recent past. Thus it is something of a modern notion itself, an irony of which few of its current exponents are fully aware. Thus, a revival of classicism is a demanding phenomenon both for those who question the value of tradition and a beacon for those who encourage it.

In 1988 Haslemere Estates completed a 120.000 square foot office retail development at Richmond Riverside with parking for one hundred and thirty-five cars. The architect was Quinlan Terry, best known, like his mentor Raymond Erith, for small country houses in the 'Georgian style'. Incorporating Heron House of 1716, some so-so 1850s buildings and the old Richmond Town Hall, Terry's brief was to use 'traditional materials' and it would be churlish to deny that with them he has achieved a dignified urban mass which sits better in the Richmond townscape than a spun aluminium and tensioned guy-wire New Town Advanced Factory Unit would have done.

But in his buildings at Richmond Riverside, Terry has departed from classicism. This is not in any sense a real classical building because the architecture is one of effect, rather than of substance. Palladio, whose *Quattro Libri* was an essentially practical book which explained how to stop a chimney smoking as well as how to design a palazzo, explained, in Wotton's version:

> "Beauty will result from the form and correspondence of the whole, with respect to the several parts, of the parts with regard for each other and of these gain to the whole; that the structure may appear an entire and complete body."

The 'harmony, balance, permanence' and so forth and all the other longed-for qualities of a classical revival are subordinated in Richmond to a commercial brief. Thus, behind the facades of 'traditional materials' there is an undistinguished late 1980s commercial development. With this disjunction between form and content, the essential disciplines of classicism have been ignored and abused.

While one of the most elegant criticisms of modern architecture was that it was all too often designed from the inside out,[2] giving the functional considerations priority over the less scientific human ones, Quinlan Terry's architecture could be said to have the opposite fault: it is designed from the outside in, putting effect before convenience. Thus it is neither an archaeological precise replica of anything in particular, nor an inspired re-interpretation. To Richard Meier, RIBA Gold Medallist in 1988, architecture of the modern 'classical revival'; "ransacks the past, robs the present and obliterates the future."[3]

2　The observation was Robert Venturi's.

3　*Architects Journal,* 2nd November 1988.

A more extreme version of culture being put to the service of commerce appears in the extraordinary buildings of Flaxyard Plc, the development company founded by Ian Pollard. For the *Observer* newspaper on a derelict site opposite London's Battersea Park, Flaxyard has built a structure which, with characteristically exotic reference, it is pleased to call Marco Polo. This is a decorated shed in the grand manner, a wonderfully vulgar — even swaggering — use of the most elemental parts of the classical language of architecture to create a building which no-one can ignore, even if they wish to, as many do.

Ian Pollard is an outsider in the closed-shop of English architecture; his views are quietly heterodox and defiantly middlebrow, but he has a shrewd understanding of the 'spirit of the age.' As a consequence, criticisms of Marco Polo have been eloquent, colourful and intense, even in the face of considerable popular interest: it has been called scaleless and coarse; ungainly; traditional; plagiarized; heavy-handed; sad; the facades mere graphics, the interiors mundane. Most interesting of all, the suggestion that Pollard's buildings are 'advertising, not architecture'.

Unconcerned by the robust reaction to his brash reinterpretation of classical architecture, Flaxyard's next major development was a new store, also in London, but this time at Earl's Court, for Sainsbury's Homebase. Both the Sainsbury family and the Sainsbury business are energetic patrons of architecture, but Sir John (now Lord) Sainsbury — the sponsor of the pseudo-classical extension of the National Gallery by American architect, Robert Venturi — was horrified when he saw his new superstore with its Egyptian gods, reliefs and murals, but — worse — its monumental screen of free-standing Corinthian columns. No matter that Venturi slapped classical pilasters on the outside of the National Gallery extension to Sir John Sainsbury's evident approval, but classical columns *outside* a supermarket evidently offended some deep-seated traditional sense of propriety, so Sir John had them pulled down. This emasculation of a *bravura* piece of architectural kitsch was clear evidence that the 'value of tradition' lobby is dismayed by the liberation of art and the deregulation of history which the comingling of commerce and culture has brought about.

There was another example with telephone booths. In November 1987 Mercury, the independent telecommunications contractor, was licensed by the British Government to compete with the British Telecom monopoly. It was to make Mercury's presence more strongly felt on the street that the brave decision was made to commission designs for new 'phone booths. The bravery, however, was not without a flavour of opportunism because, since privatisation the most public debate about the value of tradition in Britain has been concerned with British Telecom's decision to phase out the old iron booths, designed by Sir Giles Gilbert Scott, and replace them with more 'modern' ones.

To most British citizens above the age of ten, Scott's bright red 'phone booths form an essential component of the national landscape and British Telecom's decision to scrap them was a calculated offence against public taste. None but the scholarly might have realized that Scott's 'K2' design was a subtle reworking of classical motifs (including a canopy adapted from Sir John Soane's Dulwich College Picture Gallery), but the easy dignity and familiarity of the old booth was ample evidence of the capacity of the classical repertoire — in skilled hands — to satisfy popular need; 1,200 of them have been declared 'listed buildings'. In announcing the decision to compete not only in telecommunications traffic, but also in street furniture, Mercury committed itself to a debate about design. The idea was to commission three curious designs, each very different, so that 'aesthetic consideration...(can)...be to taken into account at every location', promising to change the booths in response to public opinion. The booths were quite distinct from the advanced Telecom hardware, with its LCD display, credit card facility and volume controls. Here you have the same distinction between form and content which we saw in Richmond and Cambridge and

21. Post Modernism is 'architecture as advertising'. Ian Pollard's Marco Polo building in London's Battersea reinterprets classicism to create a slick package for a newspaper publisher.

21

22 – 25. Giles Gilbert Scott's original telephone kiosk (1927) was outstanding street furniture, both traditional and original. Mercury commissioned new kiosks in 1988, the designers were (left-to-right) John Simpson, Machin Associates and Fitch & Company.

22

23

24

25

26. Ian Pollard also designed a Homebase store in London's Earl's Court (below) which used Egyptian motifs to enhance transactions between money and D.I.Y. Post Modernism liberated architectural history, but threatened meaning.

26

21

the same fascination with traditional value which appears to be characteristic of much late twentieth-century architecture. As scenery to contextualise the 'phone technology, Mercury showed that 'design' has become simply a menu of more-or-less understood ingredients, sanctioned by history: Fitch & Company, the retail design specialists, proposed 'art deco', Machin Architects offered something like a conservatory while classical architect, John Simpson designed something which he described as a monument to improve public spaces. The Simpson design was soon withdrawn because the design by Fitch had been selected for sixty British Rail Stations and BR insisted on uniformity. Besides, only a few hundred members of the public had bothered to express an opinion.[4]

4   *Building Design*, 20th January 1989.

Any discussion of the value of tradition must depend on an understanding of the question: 'Where *do* architects and designers get their ideas?' The answer, of course, is mainly from other architects and designers, so is it mere casuistry to distinguish between tradition and plagiarism? Borrowing forms and details was once the very mechanism of art, architecture and design. Nowadays copyright, patent registration and licensing prevent it. But modern conditions alter the *meaning* of borrowing.

What *exactly* is the difference between copying a Rolex and copying a Corinthian column, particularly when in each case the copying serves only to emphasise the inherent distinctions between the technical function of the original and its clone...neither Pollard's or Terry's columns nor a Taiwanese copy of a Swiss wrist-watch bear much relationship, other than superficial appearance, to their original models. That either form of counterfeit is possible, even passable, is evidence that our civilization has a slavish dedication to tradition. Seemingly, it is unable to find lasting value outside or beyond images, forms and details made familiar by custom and use.

Post Modern architecture and design is a *bricolage* of styles and allusions, an art of surface effects made possible by the deregulation of history. With its emphasis on 'packaging and reproducibility'[5] it confirms that in the Post Modern era culture is truly the handmaiden of commerce. Buildings are designed and marketed like consumer products. Architecture *is* a form of advertising. Yet the articulate lobby which promotes a new classical revival does not acknowledge its shallowness and its abuse of tradition.

5   For an eloquent account of this curious development, see Todd Gittlin's article in *The New York Times Review of Books*, 6th November 1988.

The classical defence is a conservative one. The extreme reactionary position with respect to the debate about the value of tradition was stated one hundred and eighty years ago by French architect, Charles Percier. He believed that true creativity lay in making judicious choices from what was already available, rather than struggling for meretricious novelty against the inertia of a thousand years of custom and tradition.

This is to suggest that genuine invention and creativity are undesirable, where they are not impossible, but this would be to refute any notion of real progress in design, or – indeed – in anything else. The assumption must be that those who can see value only in tradition, or versions of it, deny man's ability to adapt to changing circumstances.[6]

6   For the contrary view see Essay #19.

Now that we have technology available which makes the reproduction of any past detail, form or structure easy, now that we have the scholarly resources – and cultural inclination – to view all of history as our property, the future could well be spent in sporadic regurgitation of the designs of Bramante or Sir John Soane. We presently put so high a price on tradition because the coming together of commerce and culture has left us in a daze of confused values, with nowhere to run but the past. Morbid dread and self-indulgence are characteristic of the *fin-de-siècle*, but out of the malaise of one century ago emerged radical, new solutions to the problems of tradition or innovation in design. Nowadays, the fusion of commerce and culture makes all ideas and images available as never before. It seems likely that something genuinely new will emerge, or civilization is condemned to ceaseless reproduction of what it knows best.

MODERNISM

Dan Cruickshank

Cruickshank (*b.*1949) is features editor for the *Architects' Journal*. His special interest is Georgian architecture and he has often been represented on the boards of heritage pressure groups. His books include *Rape of Britain* (with C. Amery, 1975) and *Life in the Georgian City* (1989).

*M*odernism is, perhaps, the one great idea of the twentieth century – the one original idea that is impossible to discover in preceding ages and, indeed, is even now alien in most contemporary cultures outside Western Europe and North America.

By Modernism I mean the positive rejection of the past and the blind belief in the process of change, in novelty for its own sake, in the idea that progress through time equates with cultural progress; in the cult of individuality, originality and self-expression.

All these ideas have, of course, been present in the past, but not all together at the same time. Each generation is painfully aware of its own shortcomings and, through individuals, identifies ailments, demands changes and prescribes cures.

But only this age could produce, say, Richard Rogers' Lloyds building. Not because only we have the technology, materials, and so on, but because only we possess the desire to make Modernism manifest, to turn tradition on its head, elevating the practical nuts and bolts of building – the service ducts, lift shafts, the means of construction – into the position formally held by erudite reinterpretations of tradition and by elevations thought appropriate for the public role of architecture.

The readiness of twentieth-century architects to reject these traditions was a direct consequence of one of the major artistic events of the twentieth century – the appearance of abstraction as a real alternative to figurative art. The belief that emotions could be evoked by mere reference to form and colour with no direct association with the human body was a massive blow to the millenia old aesthetic conviction that man is the perfect prototype of proportion. Only through reference to the divine guide-lines latent in the human form and proportions could artists achieve great effects and absolute beauty. Distortion of the body was possible – as practised, for example, in Egypt – not out of naivety or incompetence (could the pyramid builders not make a naturalistic study of the human form?) but because a specific form of abstraction discovered an essence and gave meaning and emphasis. But the complete disassociation from the human body that we have seen in the twentieth century, coupled with an obsessive desire for novelty, make it only natural that traditional architecture – the human body in brick or stone should have been completely rejected by avant-garde twentieth-century architects.

One can say that contemporary buildings like Lloyd's reflect a simple dictum – a determination to express new materials and construction – a sort of architectural methodism, coolly calculating in its rational exclusion of reference to cultures not fortunate enough to have advanced technologies with which to play. But there is more to it. As revealed in Lloyd's, so called High-Tech buildings are far from merely rational expressions of construction and function; subjective aesthetics have come into play so that services are arranged in a pleasing manner, and certain elements are manufactured in more expensive materials for aesthetic effect; in short, the building becomes a theatrical demonstration of its functional ideal. In this romanticism, High-Tech

28. Lloyd's was
completed in 1986.
Conceived, by Richard
Rogers as a sophisticated
modular system, it
discomforted the clients
who depended on
traditional work practices.

28

29. Egyptian relief, with
stylized figures.

29

30. Fritz Lang's *Metropolis*
(1926) gave the cinema an
image of the future which
predicted the modern city.

30

24

architecture is, of course, no different in spirit — if totally different in form — from all romantic architecture of the past.

So what is the real appeal of Modernism, if in essence it is only old ideas stripped of those cultural and historic references that were in the past thought to be the ornaments of learning and civilization?

To generations brought up on the idea of continuity, of change by evolution not revolution, crude and overblown images of the type offered now by Modernist architects were regarded as either vulgar — for they revealed an unfamiliarity with the classical principles of harmony, proportion, beauty — or as sinister. One need only think of H. G. Wells' Things to Come (1936) or, more complex, the huge machine imagery of totalitarianism in Metropolis (1926).

Is it the building types demanded in the late twentieth century that have made the break with tradition inevitable? Can you imagine a classical airport? But then could you have imagined a Grecian or Gothic railway terminal (Euston, St Pancras), a wide span bridge in which revolutionary design combined so effectively with history (Clifton Suspension Bridge)?

If the proposition is that civilization is based on continuity of thought, of individual endeavour linked to form a chain of progress (one generation discovers, another develops, yet another perfects) and that the products of this refined process are consequently imbued with certain well tested truths, then regard for tradition can be seen as a vital ingredient in the creative process. Tradition represents a repository of experience that can be tapped at will by the knowledgeable. If it is accepted that the Modernist revolution of the early twentieth century has failed to produce an architecture of sufficient cultural richness and subtlety, then the question is how are we to reconnect with our architectural and planning tradition, to learn from history and to fuse past with present to create a convincing, unselfconscious, new architecture?

The problem is not new: most of later twentieth-century architecture is precisely to do with the bid to reconcile tradition and historicism with new building types and technology to produce an architecture that reflected the aspirations of the age. Another, perhaps more useful example, is presented by Nordic Neo-classicism of the twentieth century when really remarkable reinterpretations of traditional architecture were produced, notably by Erik Gunnar Asplund.

In fact, history is full of moments when the desire for architectural and cultural continuity was reconciled with the demand of challenging new building types. The trick is to learn the right lessons and to recognise that the creative force that was unleashed by meeting the challenge, and the change of architectural direction that the synthesis provoked, reinvigorates history and prevents a regard for tradition from being a dead hand on contemporary design.

The Roman adaptation of Greek Classicism to create new building types — multi-storey markets, gigantic baths — was one such moment, and enriched antique classicism with a new series of motifs and types of construction; the Italian Renaissance developed Roman precedent to create the building types it needed, the seventeenth and eighteenth centuries dwelt almost exclusively on the stylistic possibilities of reinterpreting history while finding established structural systems quite adequate for their new building types.

However, it is in the very early nineteenth century that we discover more relevant lessons for then, as now, new methods of construction and new materials were available for the creation of new building types.

Most dramatic are the fireproof mills and warehouses which utilised the possibility offered by new cast iron technology (wider spans, increased floor loads, speed of construction, improved fire resistance, easy repetition of units) and combined these characteristics with the prevailing taste for austere Neo-classicism to create memorable buildings that look both to the past and to the future while also being thoroughly of their age. What we need now is to combine the spatial possibilities offered by Modernism and the constructional possibilities offered by new materials and building technologies with traditional virtues. Modernism has not produced a vocabulary for dealing with elevations (as the current batch of frightful commercial 'stick on' elevations reveal) if the mere expression of construction or display of technical gadgetry is not acceptable; nor has it offered a way of making cities that even compare with the civic achievements of the past.

Ways of using history must be re-discovered significant ways, not just the Post-Modern option of cladding a functional frame with stick on pediments. This is the great challenge of the next decade and must be met if architecture is once again to become a popular art without having to stoop to popularism, and if it is to fulfil the aspirations of both the architectural profession and the users of architecture.

31. Erik Gunnar
Asplaud's Stockholm
Library
(1921-8) is an example of
refined classicism.

32. Warehouse, in
Tobacco Dock.

33. Gothic detail at
St Pancras, London
(1863-76).

31

33

32

34

34. Trajan's Market,
Rome (*c.*100-112 AD).

35. Different claddings
being considered for Cesar
Pelli at Canary Wharf
while construction
proceeds in the
background, 1989.

35

27

36. The famous Apollo
Belvedere, a masterpiece of
Classical sculpture, and a
source of inspiration for the
Neo-classicists, is only a
copy of the original.

37. Domenico Brucciani, from
a shop in Covent Garden
turned the history of
sculpture into a business
selling plaster casts.

37

36

38

38. Owen Jones' *Grammar of
Ornament* (1856) was one
of the first books to
formulate a theory of design
which encouraged invention
rather than tradition.

39. The most famous image of
the Second World War,
raising the flag at Iwo Jima,
was faked. It was invention,
not observation.

39

REPRODUCTIONS
AND ORIGINALS

Why do we still, almost instinctively, confer greater value on original works of art than on reproductions? What does this distinction tell us in an age of mass production of everything where image, form and sound can be instantly captured, recorded and reproduced, when everything is potentially available, ephemeral, and almost free? Two parts of the answers are clear: technologies or reproduction bring into question the *value* of tradition and the special status of art.[1] In industrial societies, the very notion of *design* is dependent on the potential to reproduce ideas, images and objects.

[1] See Essay #7.

There is nothing new about the idea of reproducing works of art. The celebrated Apollo Belvedere, considered by Winckelmann to be "the highest ideal of art" and thereby becoming the touchstone of eighteenth-century values, is itself a reproduction. Here we have a work of art, understood for more than two hundred years to be the maximum expression of nobility attainable in sculpture, which is not even in its true medium: the statue now in the Vatican is no more than a Roman marble copy of an original Greek bronze. What is more, the copy was made some five hundred years later.[2] The history of its reproduction is as absurd as if a cast-iron Victorian copy of a medieval sculpture had had a decisive, even formative, influence on the development of modern art.

[2] The original, which is thought to have stood in the agora at Athens, was probably made by Leochares c.330-320 BC. The marble copy was brought by Pope Julius II from his palazzo at San Pietro in Vincoli to the Belvedere of the Vatican.

Yet copying works of art was not alien to the nineteenth century. In painting, the process was formalised by the French Academy in Rome where Colbert insisted that the students copy "everything beautiful", thus creating a seventeenth-century manufactory for works of art. Two hundred years later thousands of copies of greater and minor pictures had been commissioned to furnish the *bureaux* of all ranks of the French Administration from Djibouti to Calais.

[3] In the *Dictionnaire de l'Academie des Beaux-Arts*, 1858, 'copie' is defined as "wrestling from Genius its secret".

In the *ateliers* of the Academy copying was considered a valuable stimulus to the creative imagination, not a substitute for it. Since it was thought a copyist could possibly improve on the original,[3] copying became the second most important discipline after drawing from life models, where all the students were expected to do was improve on nature. Major copies were housed in the Musée des Etudes for the instruction of students, the Academy putting a high price on diligence. Eventually in 1874 an actual Musée des Copies was established, housing one hundred and fifty-six copies of masterpieces. This venture was the less curious if it is emphasized that an educational system which values diligent study as much as 'creativity', just as it prefers technique to interpretation, was able to consider the contents of the Musée des Copies as works of art in their own right.

This notion of copying appealed to the bureaucratic French mind, which also graded painters and supported them with commissions. The French Academy's formal institution of copying was characteristic of a nation's preoccupation with cultural bureaucracy. At the same time in London, a similar museum of copies was established which was equally characteristic of its host nation's preoccupation with commerce.

[4] Brucciani was born in 1815, came to London c.1830; and died there in 1880.

Domenico Brucciani[4] ran a successful plaster cast business in Russell Street, Covent Garden. In a sense one of the descendents of the itinerant, jobbing *stuccatori* so familiar with the British building trade in the eighteenth century, Brucciani busily adapted his craft from artisan decoration of houses (already industrialized by the nineteenth century) to purposes better suited to the demands of their age. Since 1841 the Government Schools of Design had been collecting casts of statuary and even had a 'keeper' responsible for them; Brucciani made his business the supply of casts to the burgeoning system of British art schools, a trade which flourished well into 1950s.[5]

[5] Although when the original Brucciani business neared collapse in 1919, it was taken over by the Victoria and Albert Museum.

In 1864 Brucciani opened a unique institution, part shop, part museum...his 'Galleria dell Bell Arti' which contained copies of the finest statuary in existence, at least according to contemporary taste. Widely reported in all the art journals, Brucciani's 'Galleria' was both a showroom for the sale of merchandise as well as an educational experience for its inquisitive visitors.

It was Brucciani who cast the Portico de la Gloria at Santiago de Compostela in 1866,[6] still one of the most technically remarkable and physically impressive of specimens in the Victoria and Albert Museum's Cast Courts. These were solemn walls, so redolent of the traditional horror and evening of museums, were a live issue in the mid to later nineteenth century, not least because they tested so many assumptions about the value of art and the relationship of that value to its educational, or even aesthetic, worth. The painter, Ingres, for instance, had had doubts about the system of copying employed by the French Academy since he believed, rather like Owen Jones,[7] that the mysterious essence of a masterpiece did not lie in mere details. But for the new middle classes, ignorant of the theory of art, negligent in connoisseurship, cast courts were a special attraction. In New York, the Metropolitan Museum had a Hall of Casts which, hubristically, included the Parthenon and the hypostyle hall from Karnak.

[6] G. E. Street's *Account of Gothic Architecture in Spain*, 1865, had used an illustration of the Portico as a frontispiece.

[7] In his monumental *The Grammar of Ornament*, 1856, Jones declared that "I have ventured to hope that, in thus bringing into immediate juxtaposition the many forms of beauty which every style of ornament presents, I might aid in arresting that unfortunate tendency of our time to be content with copying..."

Certain fine artists may have felt threatened by the prospect of art being licensed, copied and distributed in the form of reproductions, but the practice had eloquent champions, including George Wallis, the Keeper of the Art Collection in the South Kensington Museum. Wallis had noticed that the expansion of museums would mean that eventually the demand for art would outpace the supply. He explained:

> "As personal wealth increases, and taste for collecting extends, the private buyer comes into the market...as museums increase, they also become competitors, chiefly with each other."[8]

[8] In *Transactions of the National Association for the Advancement of Art and its Application to Industry*, 1888.

Wallis' rationale for using reproductions was that the study of them would improve popular taste at modest cost, but this canny commercial observation was not his only conviction, since he was intellectually committed to the idea of using copies in education. He scorned the connoisseur, with his fetishistic, precious demand for the unique and wrote a stirring defence of the very modern notion that quality in art is quite independent of uniqueness:

> "Nothing to the true lover of art can appear more absurd than the worship of intrinsic value, and the neglect of that extrinsic value which comes from the beauty of form, proportion and adaptation to use."[9]

[9] ibid.

While it is tempting to interpret Wallis' arguments as a prophetic defence of industrial design as a genuinely popular art, to do so would be an error in historical method. What Wallis' interpretation of the role of the Cast Courts does represent is an early expression of an idea which was to gain currency in the twentieth century: new technologies, in John Berger's words, make art "ephemeral, ubiquitous, insubstantial, available, valueless, free."[10]

[10] In *Ways of Seeing*, 1972.

This liberation of art from 'value' was a fundamental part of the ideologies of the various modern movements, most of which attacked both the bogus respect for pictures and their preciousness in the market-place. This stigmatisiation of painting allowed design to flourish as a major — perhaps *the* major — creative discipline. Bogus respect and market value, they said, were mere replacements for that magical quality which painting lost as soon as photography was invented.

The most eloquent spokesman for the persuasive idea that photography, the most efficient and universal of the new reproduction technologies, had robbed traditional art of meaning and value was Walter Benjamin, a social critic belonging to the Frankfurt School. Benjamin was obsessed by the parallel development of photography and socialism and felt that each fed off one another. Enthused by the evocative stills of Eugene Atget and the heroic movies of Abel Gance, Benjamin wrote an influential essay called 'The Work of Art in the Age of Mechanical Reproduction'.[11] Here he argued that the emergence of photography and film suddenly robbed images of any 'cult' value and, instead, promoted secular, insubstantial, images for popular scrutiny. It is not so much that photography and film (and he might also have added, industrial design) are necessarily arts in their own right, but that their invention changed the entire nature of art.

Benjamin took his own life at the beginning of the Second World War, so did not live to witness an extraordinary phenomenon which both validated his conviction about the universal appeal of photographic images, but also supplied powerful evidence on the contrariness of human nature which, even against powerful rational arguments, finds comfort and delight in the bogus. The story of the most famous photographic image of the War proves that it is only a short distance from reproduction to fake.

The 28th Marines of the 5th Division were ordered to take Mt. Suribachi, an extinct volcano on Iwo Jima. After a bloody exchange, resolved in the favour of the Americans, a lieutenant was given a small flag and a length of pipe to act as a flagpole. The makeshift assemblage was erected as the victory celebration and that would have been that, cult value and all, until a photographer of the Associated Press news agency, one Joe Rosenthal, decided a picture opportunity was being wasted, so he came up the slope with a larger flag and another team. They had some difficulty erecting the now huge flag, so the original detail joined in and, there you had it, a stage-managed image, a styled photograph, which became a symbol of the United States Pacific war effort. The same picture was used for the 7th War Loans fund raising drive and served as the model for the largest bronze statue in the world, the Marine Corps Memorial in Arlington, Virginia. The Mt. Suribachi anecdotes closed the gap between reproductions and fakes, providing wry proof of Benjamin's theory that the invention of photography changed the nature of art.

There was a moment in the nineteenth century, somewhere about the time when the great museums and the great department stores were being opened, when the poster ceased to be a straightforward broadsheet of printed information, and became a mixed-media advertisement, using illustration and copy to create an effect which was more than merely workaday. Henri de Toulouse-Lautrec and Jules Cheret are familiar as creators of the 'art poster' and the tradition they established has continued through the century. The value of the reproducible *image*, as opposed to the value of an 'authentic' original is articulately defended by Milton Glaser, when he says

"Why don't we discard the word 'art' and replace it with the word 'work'?"[12]

The concept 'fake' tests many of the rooted prejudices we have of culture. The very idea makes assumptions about authenticity, which are undermined by developments

11 See Essay #6.

12 See Essay #8.

40, 41. With Toulouse-Lautrec and Jules Cheret, paintings were reproduced into commercial art.

41

40

42

42, 43. Industrial design depends on reproduction, questioning the value of originality. Le Corbusier's *Grand Confort* has been continuously reproduced since 1928. Edwin Lutyens' *Napoleon* chair (1919) was revived in 1988.

43

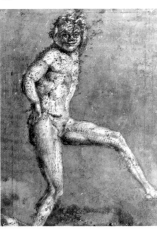

44.

44. Umberto Eco warned against condemning fakes or marginal expressions of culture, saying celebrated Pompeian frescoes were originally just advertisements for brothels.

in twentieth-century technology and design. Mass-produced design, whether of a poster or a product, makes a nonsense of the prejudice against fakes.

The concept of authenticity has moved on, no longer is it inherent in a unique original, for when Ford produces hundreds of thousands of Escorts every year it is clearly nonsensical to talk in terms of reproduction or original. Instead, today we have piracy. No-one has yet made a counterfeit Ford Escort (not least because the initial investment in tooling would render the project financially inefficient, given Ford's own commitment to selling global products), but counterfeits of more technically simple products are abundant. That there is demand for fake watches, fake luggage and fake furniture is evidence of human bondage to tradition, although in this case tradition of a novel sort. It is also evidence that our contemporaries value the authority of brand names: as the cost of hardware tumbles, the aura of famous names, including Cartier, Rolex, Vuitton and Hermes, begins to acquire value, hence unscrupulous piracy and counterfeiting.

It is a beguiling paradox that companies such as IBM, whose growth has depended on the vitality of mass-production businesses, now spends £30m every year to protect its secrets.[13] Similarly, the furniture manufacturer, Cassina, which owns the rights to manufacture Le Corbusier's design, says that his designs were never intended for 'commercial reproduction', a declaration that seems to run entirely contrary to the architect's own beliefs about the role of design and products in the modern world.

So, there are two forces in conflict, or, at least, in tension. One is the universality of design in the modern world, the other is the need of the manufacturers to protect their property, even when that property is an idea or an image rather than, say, real estate. It was the simultaneous development of the department store and the museum in the middle of the nineteenth century which gave rise to them.

[13] According to the Counterfeiting Intelligence Bureau of the International Chamber of Commerce.

45

45, 46. Walter Benjamin argued that photography and film changed the nature of art. A scene from Abel Gance's *Napoleon* (1927) and Leonardo's *Mona Lisa* (1505-1514), the most reproduced – yet most revered – of paintings, Benjamin wanted to know why we prefer the original, when copies can be as good.

46

THE WORK OF ART IN THE AGE OF MECHANICAL REPRODUCTION
Walter Benjamin

Benjamin (1892-1940) wrote *The Concept of Art Criticism in German Romanticism* and *The Origin of German Tragedy*, but he is best known for this essay on art and photography, originally published as 'Das Kunstwerk im Zeitalten seinen Technischen Reproduzierbarkeit' in *Zeitschrift fur Sozialforschung*. Benjamin's perceptions were influenced by Marx, but his observations on the relationship of technology, creativity and value were entirely original and have been immensely influential on the succeeding generation of critics.

In principle a work of art has always been reproducible. Man-made artefacts could always be imitated by men. Replicas were made by pupils in practice of their craft, by masters for diffusing their works, and, finally, by third parties in the pursuit of gain. Mechanical reproduction of a work of art, however, represents something new. Historically, it advanced intermittently and in leaps at long intervals, but with accelerated intensity. The Greeks knew only two procedures for technically reproducing works of art: founding and stamping. Bronzes, terracottas, and coins were the only art works which they could produce in quantity. All others were unique and could not be mechanically reproduced. With the woodcut graphic art became mechanically reproducible for the first time, long before script became reproducible by print.

For the first time in the process of pictorial reproduction, photography freed the hand of the most important artistic functions which henceforth devolved only upon the eye looking into a lens. Since the eye perceives more swiftly than the hand can draw, the process of pictorial reproduction was accelerated so enormously that it could keep pace with speech.

A film operator shooting a scene in the studio captures the images at the speed of an actor's speech. Just as lithography virtually implied the illustrated newspaper, so did photography foreshadow the sound film. The technical reproduction of sound was tackled at the end of the last century. Around 1900 technical reproduction had reached a standard that not only permitted it to reproduce all transmitted works of art and thus to cause the most profound change in their impact upon the public; it also had captured a place of its own among the artistic processes. For the study of this standard nothing is more revealing than the nature of the repercussions that these two different manifestations — the reproduction of works of art and the art of the film — have had on art in its traditional form.

The presence of the original is the prerequisite to the concept of authenticity. Chemical analysis of the patina of a bronze can help to establish this, as does the proof that a given manuscript of the Middle Ages stems from an archive of the fifteenth century. The whole sphere of authenticity is outside technical reproducibility. Confronted with its manual reproduction, which was usually branded as a forgery, the original preserved all its authority; not so vis à vis technical reproduction.

The reason is twofold. First, process reproduction is more independent of the original than manual reproduction. For example, in photography, process reproduction can bring out those aspects of the original that are unattainable to the naked eye yet accessible to the lens, which is adjustable and chooses its angle at will. And photographic reproduction, with the aid of certain processes, such as enlargement or slow motion, can capture images which escape natural vision. Secondly, technical reproduction can put the copy of the original into situations which would be out of reach for the original itself. Above all, it enables the original to meet the beholder halfway, be it in the form of a photograph or a phonograph record. The cathedral leaves its locale to be received in the studio of a lover of art; the choral production, performed in an auditorium or in the open air, resounds in the drawing room.

The situations into which the product of mechanical reproduction can be brought may not touch the actual work of art, yet the quality of its presence is always depreciated. This holds not only for art but also, for instance, for a landscape which passes in review before the spectator in a movie. In the case of the art object, a most sensitive nucleus — namely, its authenticity — is interfered with whereas no natural object is vulnerable on that score. The authenticity of a thing is the essence of all that is transmissible from its beginning, ranging from its substantive duration to its testimony to the history which it has experienced. Since the historical testimony rests on the authenticity, the former, too, is jeopardized by reproduction when substantive duration ceases to matter. And what is really jeopardized when the historical testimony is affected is the authority of the object.

The uniqueness of a work of art is inseparable from its being embedded in the fabric of tradition. This tradition itself is thoroughly alive and extremely changeable. An ancient statue of Venus, for example, stood in a different traditional context with the Greeks, who made it an object of veneration, than with the clerics of the Middle Ages, who viewed it as an ominous idol. Both of them, however, were equally confronted with its uniqueness, that is, its aura. Originally the contextual integration of art in tradition found its expression in the cult. We know that the earliest art works originated in the service of a ritual — first the magical, then the religious kind.

It is significant that the existence of the work of art with reference to its aura is never entirely separated from its ritual function. In other words, the unique value of the 'authentic' work of art has its basis in ritual, the location of its original use value. This ritualistic basis, however remote, is still recognizable as secularized ritual even in the most profane forms of the cult of beauty. The secular cult of beauty, developed during the Renaissance and prevailing for three centuries, clearly showed that ritualistic basis in its decline and the first deep crisis which befell it. With the advent of the first truly revolutionary means of reproduction, photography, simultaneously with the rise of socialism, art sensed the approaching crisis which has become evident a century later. At the time, art reacted with the doctrine of l'art pour l'art, that is, with a theology of art. This gave rise to what might be called a negative theology in the form of the idea of 'pure' art, which not only denied any social function of art but also any categorizing by subject matter.

An analysis of art in the age of mechanical reproduction must do justice to these relationships for they lead us to an all-important insight: for the first time in world history, mechanical reproduction emancipates the work of art from its parasitical dependence on ritual. To an ever greater degree the work of art reproduced becomes the work of art designed for reproducibility. From a photographic negative, for example, one can make any number of prints; to ask for the 'authentic' print makes no sense. But the instant the criterion of authenticity ceases to be applicable to artistic productions, the total function of art is reversed. Instead of being based on ritual, it begins to be based on another practice — politics.

Works of art are received and valued on different planes. Two polar types stand out:

with one, the accent is on the cult value; with the other, on the exhibition value of the work. Artistic production begins with ceremonial objects destined to serve in a cult. One may assume that what mattered was their existence, not their being on view. The elk portrayed by the man of the Stone Age on the walls of his cave was an instrument of magic. He did expose it to his fellow men, but in the main it was meant for the spirits. Today the cult value would seem to demand that the work of art remain hidden. Certain statues of gods are accessible only to the priest in the cella; certain Madonnas remain covered nearly all year round; certain sculptures on medieval cathedrals are invisible to the spectator on ground level. With the emancipation of the various art practices from ritual go increasing opportunities for the exhibition of their products. It is easier to exhibit a portrait bust that can be sent here and there than to exhibit the statue of a divinity that has its fixed place in the interior of a temple. The same holds for the painting as against the mosaic or fresco that preceded it. And even though the public presentability of a mass originally may have been just as great as that of a symphony, the latter originated at the moment when its public presentability promised to surpass that of the mass.

With the different methods of technical reproduction of a work of art, its fitness for exhibition increased to such an extent that the quantitative shift between its two poles turned into a qualitative transformation of its nature. This is comparable to the situation of the work of art in prehistoric times when, by the absolute emphasis on its cult value, it was first, and foremost, an instrument of magic. Only later did it come to be recognized as a work of art. In the same way today, by the absolute emphasis on its exhibition value the work of art becomes a creation with entirely new functions, among which the one we are conscious of, the artistic function, later may be recognized as incidental. This much is certain: today photography and film are the most serviceable exemplifications of this new function.

In photography, exhibition value begins to displace cult value along the line. But cult value does not give way without resistance. It retires into an ultimate retrenchment: the human countenance. It is no accident that the portrait was the focal point of early photography. The cult of remembrance of loved ones, absent or dead, offers a last refuge for the cult value of the picture. For the last time the aura emanates from the early photographs in the fleeting expression of a human face. This is what constitutes their melancholy, incomparable beauty. But as man withdraws from the photographic image, the exhibition value for the first time shows its superiority to the ritual value.

To have pin-pointed this new stage constitutes the incomparable significance of Atget, who, around 1900, took photographs of deserted Paris streets. It has quite justly been said of him that he photographed them like scenes of crime. The scene of a crime too, is deserted; it is photographed for the purpose of establishing evidence. With Atget, photographs become standard evidence for historical occurrences, and acquire a hidden political significance. They demand a specific kind of approach; free-floating contemplation is not appropriate to them. They stir the viewer; he feels challenged by them in a new way. At the time picture magazines begin to put up signposts for him, right ones or wrong ones, no matter. For the first time, captions have become obligatory. And it is clear that they have an altogether different character than the title of a painting.

The nineteenth-century dispute as to the artistic value of painting versus photography today seems devious and confused. This does not diminish its importance, however, if anything, it underlines it. Earlier much futile thought had been devoted to the question of whether photography is an art. The primary question – whether the very invention of photography had not transformed the entire nature of art – was not raised.

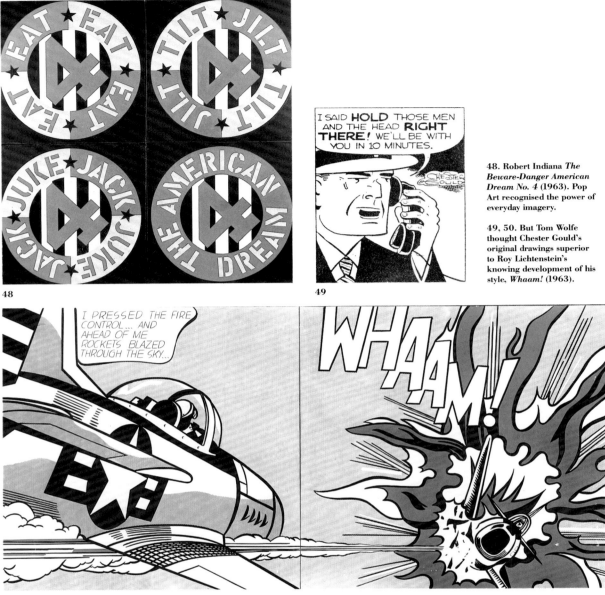

48

49

48. Robert Indiana *The Beware-Danger American Dream No. 4* (1963). Pop Art recognised the power of everyday imagery.

49, 50. But Tom Wolfe thought Chester Gould's original drawings superior to Roy Lichtenstein's knowing development of his style, *Whaam!* (1963).

50

51, 52. Tom Wolfe also believed that in the American strip, quality graphics like Raymond Loewy's Union 76 globes achieved the status of art.

52

51

CHESTER GOULD VERSUS ROY LICHTENSTEIN

Tom Wolfe

Wolfe (*b*.1931), with Hunter S. Thompson, invented the New Journalism, and became one of the most frequently and badly imitated living writers. With its fast prose, sharp descriptions and its — sometimes ironic — celebration of the ephemeral, *The Electric Kool-Aid Acid Test* (1968) perfectly captures the character of America in the age of Pop. But Wolfe enjoys roasting sacred cows and his lampoons of Modern Art and architecture (*The Painted Word*, 1975; and *From Bauhaus to Our House*, 1981) prefigured Post Modernism. This characteristically irreverent essay playing off art against popular culture was originally contributed to an exhibition at Los Angeles County Museum.

Frankly, I would like to see the term popular culture disappear from the language. It never fails to bring darkness and gibberish down upon anyone who tries to use it. Once a visual phenomenon is categorized as part of popular culture, this is a signal to everyone in the art world that it is not necessary to take it seriously, although one is perfectly free to enjoy it in the spirit of Camp or nostalgia for the mud. This was precisely the spirit of Pop Art. The Pop artists operated on the level of Carl van Vechten visiting Harlem in the 1920s and writing Nigger Heaven. *Warhol, Lichtenstein, Oldenburg, Indiana, and the rest brought back comic strip panels, Campbell soup cans, Brillo boxes, Rexall drug store boys' first basemen's mitts, and neon signs in the spirit of anthropologists returning with tribal masks. They were capturing the world of high culture the icons created by energetic but unsophisticated and nameless artisans who did commercial designs for the populace...out there. It was on this point, however — namely, sophistication — that Pop Art ran into problems.*

Too often the artisans whose work the Pop artists adapted or copied were not unsophisticated (nor, for that matter, nameless). I can remember a show that Andy Warhol and several artists put on at the old Bianchini Gallery in New York. It was called Supermarket, *and they attempted to turn the interior of the gallery into a sophisticated version of the fluorescent glare and serial repetition (of packages, apples, cauliflowers, bottles and so on) of a supermarket. The result was something curiously pallid, however, and the show sank without a bubble. In fact, the show itself was unsophisticated. By the 1960s supermarket interiors were being put together by highly sophisticated designers and electrical engineers whose aims were rather similar to an artist's: originality, surprise, impact, careful (even if bizarre) combinations of light and colour, and stimulation of the unconscious. When it came to creating a sculptural interior using electric light and the serial repetition of forms, they knew more than Warhol and his associates and were more expert in using the available materials and techniques. In short, they were more sophisticated.*

One has only to compare the comic strip pictures of Chester Gould (Dick Tracy) *with those of Lichtenstein to see the same point illustrated. When it comes to the decisive use of line, when it comes to combining chiaroscuro and blocs of primary colours in two dimensions (perspective is of little use in the small space of a comic strip panel), Gould is more expert and more sophisticated than Lichtenstein. This is not meant as a negative statement about Lichtenstein, whose work I personally enjoy (although not as much as Gould's). After all, Gould has had far more experience. In any event, where Gould excels, it is as an artist and not as a purveyor of 'popular culture'. Once, while driving along an elevated stretch of the Santa Monica Freeway in Los Angeles at dusk, I was struck by the sight of the thousands of glowing objects that seemed to float above the landscape. Most of these were electric signs or symbols that were struck up in the air on standards precisely so they could be seen from automobiles. The most striking of all, it seemed to me, were the orange and blue UNION 76 balls revolving like big lit-up basketballs over service stations all over the city.*

Somehow a vast electric orange ball galaxy had been created forty feet above the Los Angeles basin. I set about what I figured would be the difficult search to find out what nameless and unsophisticated artisan had inadvertently succeeded in creating his own starscape over L. A. in this fashion. His name turned out to be Raymond Loewy. Raymond Loewy is probably the best-known commercial designer in America. Very little that Raymond Loewy does is inadvertent. He had thought out 'Floating Electric Orange and Blue Basketballs Over Los Angeles' down to the last watt of light and inch of elevation. Again, I have personally enjoyed the work of many serious artists who have tried to take art out into 'the environment' in a big way. But I would urge all of them, even Christo, to spend a year at the knee of Raymond Loewy, to learn from him not as Loewy the technician but as Loewy the artist.

During the 1960s art-minded friends of mine used to like to point out, with great 'pop cult' delight, certain gasoline stations in Los Angeles, and especially the Union 76 station in Beverly Hills at Santa Monica Boulevard and Crescent Drive. This station looks like some sort of Futurama Pagoda. Actually it is a huge spherical triangle resting on three piers with curving soffits lined with fluorescent strips of colour. It turned out to be by another well-known designer, Jim Wong of Pereira Associates. What Wong has done here with electric-light sculpture — as an artist — goes so far beyond what serious light sculptors like Billy Apple and Dan Flavin (and serious architects, for that matter) have yet attempted; it poses a serious question for art historians.

I would like to make the modest suggestion that in more areas of contemporary art, commercial designers are now a good decade ahead of serious (i.e. fashionable) artists — as artists — and if we are serious about art history we will record their names as their work pops up in the amazing tableaux of Los Angeles and other American cities...and will not consign them to the oblivion of popular culture. The very term 'popular culture' has unconsciously become a wall protecting serious art from the competition of the more sophisticated and gifted creatures, the platinum huns, as it were, in the...world out there...

COMMERCIAL ART
Milton Glaser

Glaser (*b*.1929) is the most celebrated graphic designer in the United States. A founder, with Seymour Chwast, of the Push Pin Studio, he is best known for his poster designs. Glaser trained with the painter, Giorgio Morandi, and is an articulate spokesman for the value of 'commercial art'.

Q: What is the commercial / artistic / social role of the poster?

A: *If we mean by 'role' a pre-existing, intrinsic function, the poster's role is to convey information from a source to an audience, in order to move that audience to an amplification or change of perception that produces an awareness or an action. When a poster has a commercial intention it obviously intends to convince an audience to buy goods and services.*

The artistic role of any poster is more difficult to ascertain. Depending on your definition, posters do not have to be 'artistic' to be effective (i.e. be successful in its 'roles'). It is far more important for posters to be effective than artistic. The aesthetic part of poster making has more to do with the objectives of its maker than the requirements of form. Because of the poster's historical relationship to the world of painting, and by virtue of its physical size, the poster seems to offer more opportunities for the designer to do artistic or imaginative work than many of the other areas in which he may be working.

In addition to the significant function of informing and motivating a public, the question of the poster's social role is a more subtle one. Does society benefit from experiencing works that have 'artistic' merit and which are well made? Without beginning to define those evasive terms I would have to say, yes, although I would be hard pressed to prove a case. To add to the ambiguity, it should be noted that a well made object may have little artistic merit, and an artistic object does not have to be well made.

Q: What do you think of the old-fashioned term 'commercial art' (*vis-à-vis* 'graphic design')?

A: *Design seems to occupy a place between fine art and craft, between aesthetics and commerce, beauty and persuasion, novelty and familiarity, and so on. Obviously, the emphasis between the polarities changes in response to the specific problem, and the intention and talent of the designer. The term 'commercial art' is a simplification and seems to eliminate the inherent conflict. For this reason I prefer the more ambiguous phrase, 'graphic design'.*

Q: Is money a corrupting influence in poster design?

A: *Perhaps in one sense: when financial risks are greatest, clients tend to be most conservative. The fear of losing a significant amount of money can have a chilling effect on one's sense of adventure and imagination.*

Q: What is your view of the poster and its relation to 'high art'?

A: *When does 'high art' meet 'low art'? At this encounter is everything above the line 'art' and everything below 'non-art'? What shall we call the material below the line craft, applied art, commercial art, decoration? Who invented this question? Who is*

CHARVOZ

55, 56. Milton Glaser's posters have a graphic simplicity that belies their artistic sophistication.

served by the distinction? Does it matter? The search for 'high art' is a theological issue, like the search for the true cross. The culture priests attempt to protect the world from false religion or faith, a never ending task. I have a modest proposal; why don't we discard the word 'art' and replace it with the word 'work'? Those objects made with care and extraordinary talent we can call 'great work', those deserving special attention, but not breathtaking, we call 'good work'. Honest, appropriately made objects without special distinction we name 'work' alone. And what remains deserves the title 'bad work'. One simple fact encourages me in this proposal; we value a good rug, a beautiful book, or a good poster over any bad painting.

Q: Does mass reproduction diminish the value of posters (i.e. does the value in matters of the visual depend on the uniqueness of the masterpieces)?

A: I seem to be getting terribly Talmudic, but it depends on one's definition of value; the most significant value of any work of art or design is in its effect on the world. Mass reproduction is one way for these works to be seen and experienced. Of course, this has nothing to do with the selling price of scarce objects. In the first case we are talking about the value of art in a cultural and historical sense, in the second we're talking about the manipulations and illusions of the market-place.

SHOPS

The moving forces behind high-consumption capitalism are the distribution of goods and the promotion of desire.

As ancient crafts and trades of the British Midlands became industrialized in the middle of the eighteenth century, with pottery ceasing to be seasonal, winter work and metalworking becoming the province of factories rather than blacksmiths, the new, efficient industries were soon making more than they could sell and it became necessary to stimulate sales. This was especially the case with ceramics; as British potters did not enjoy state, or, say, ducal patronage, they had to be especially entrepreneurial.

Two developments helped them increase demand: the catalogue and the showroom and each evolved in sympathy with the other. Cabinet-makers had established the idea of publishing directories,[1] offering designs for anyone to adapt, but at the same time advertising that there was furniture available that was ready made. But given the technology of the eighteenth century, ceramics were more immediately adaptable to mass production than furniture.

[1] Thomas Chippendale's *Gentleman and Cabinet-Maker's Directory*, 1754, is typical.

Josiah Wedgwood founded his pottery in 1759 when the practice was to send batches of his production either to merchants or to markets, but by opening showrooms in London and elsewhere, Wedgwood introduced the radical new idea of *speculative consumption*. Hitherto, the purchase of goods had required commitment and extensive negotiation by both parties, but in these new showrooms customers could inspect samples and study catalogues (or pattern books), and the proprietor might anticipate that precise orders would follow. Demand was evidently international, since between 1773 and 1788 Wedgwood's catalogues appeared with texts in English, French, German and Dutch and, as early as 1765, Wedgwood had remarked that the Americans were inclined to prefer more elaborate and expensive designs.

This first method of distance selling required not only a large range of designs, but also a considerable degree of technical discipline. The creamware patterns which became Wedgwood's stock-in-trade were of a simple design which expressed an elegant compromise of commerce and culture in that they were both an expression of the proprietor's taste, and a workable solution to the problem of mass production. Such was the effect of Wedgwood's innovations on European culture that, when searching for a means of describing the dimensions of Goethe's genius, the poet Novalis compared the polymath to the potter.[2]

[2] See Herbert Read *Art and Industry*, 1934.

Wedgwood knew that shops depend on the idea of *reproducibility* but they also depended on efficient display. In *Sketches by Boz* (1836) Dickens describes the new London fad of plate glass shopfronts.[3] Glazing emphasized the display role of the shop and after duty on glass was repealed in 1845, shop design was liberated. Asprey's is characteristic of what could be achieved in the 1850s, as was Owen Jones' shop for Osler's in Oxford Street of 1858, a design whose barrel vault betrays some influence from the Crystal Palace.

[3] Many of which are illustrated in John Tallis, *London Street Views*, 1838-9.

The transition from the individual shop, or even groups of shops in arcades or bazaars, into the more sophisticated department store is one of the crucial institutional transitions of the nineteenth century, entailing as it does necessarily more sophisticated structures with more sophisticated bureaucracy, standardized book-keeping and

4 Improved taxonomy was necessary, given William Whiteley's definition of a department store as a place where you could buy either a pin or an elephant, or anything in between.

5 It is fascinating to observe that Schinkel's designs for a museum are tantalisingly close to his designs for a *Kaufhaus*, or 'store'.

6 The *magasins de nouveautes* were established in the 1830s. The 'Ville de Paris' was the biggest of the 1840s, employing one hundred and fifty people. They were transitional institutions between merchants and department stores, pioneering free entry and an agreeable atmosphere.

7 The Bon Marché and its proprietor were the source of Emile Zola's novel, *Au Bonheur des Dames*, 1883; see Essay #10. The store was so remarkable that in his book, *Le Mécanisme de la Vie Moderne*, 1896, Georges d'Avenel devoted an entire chapter to it, see Essay #11.

8 In *Elements et Theorie de l'Architecture*, 1902.

taxonomy to support it.[4] Perhaps even more significant is the change this transition wrought on the customer. Before about 1850 the middle class were stigmatized as the *bourgeois*; after the creation of the department stores, the simple bourgeois became the more complex...*consumer*.

Although architects, including the great German Neo-classicist Karl-Friedrich Schinkel, had proposed designs for huge shops in the early years of the nineteenth century,[5] the creation of the department store is essentially a French phenomenon, just as the catalogue showroom was British.

With the department store and its implied commitment to mass production, products became commodities, just as after the invention of photography, works of art became images. The store revolutionized the process of buying, turning it into a cultural activity, rather than a reflexive response to the demands of subsistence. But it is also true that the new stores created demand as much as merely satisfying it.

The first department store to deserve the name was the Bon Marché in Paris, the creation of Aristide Boucicaut, who had been a salesman in Le Petit St Thomas, one of the *magasins de nouveautes* in the rue du Bac.[6] He started to develop his own business in 1852 and in 1869 he commissioned the architect, M. A. Laplanche to design a purpose-built store at the corner of the rue de Sèvres and the rue Velpeau. Eventually, the Bon Marché grew to occupy the entire block and Gustave Eiffel was among the distinguished architects and engineers called in to design and build extensions.[7] Eiffel had previously worked on the construction of the 1867 Paris Exposition buildings, with architect Louis-Charles Boileau and it seems not too fanciful to suggest that, as Owen Jones may have put something of the Crystal Palace into an Oxford Street shop, so Eiffel may have had a great exhibition in mind when he added to the Bon Marché.

Boucicaut's innovations, apart from the novelty of his ambition, were fixed prices, clear display, a system of exchanges and the preference for a small profit in favour of a large turnover. To observe these small distinctions is more than a mere footnote to the history of business, but far more importantly they mark a significant passage from pre-industrial barter to industrialized consumption. The idea of speculative consumerism which Wedgwood's showroom initiated was further advanced by Parisian window-shopping and the promenading encouraged by the spacious boulevards.

People were so struck by the majesty and novelty of the department stores that they were constantly looking for imagery to express their sense of awe. Zola compared them to a church ("cathédrale de commerce moderne"), but the architect and polytechnician, Julien Guadet said more interestingly that they were "musée(s) de marchandise",[8] thus, initiating the simile that led to the more recent conviction that the department store is the poor man's museum. Indeed, Boucicaut intended that the Bon Marché should excite emotions and responses similar to those excited by art: the consumers were meant to marvel and admire, as well as buy.

Zola's imaginary store, like a cathedral, offered tours, a buffet and concerts. Boucicaut's real one even included an art gallery: while the museums taught their visitors about the aristocratic taste of earlier generations, the department store allowed its consumers to mimic their habits and attire and their tastes. In this respect alone it is worth emphasizing that, like Potin, Cognaq, and other entrepreneurs who founded the great Parisian stores, Boucicaut had risen from the peasant classes.

The Bon Marché had many imitators, in France and abroad, including Au Louvre, Printemps, La Samaritaine, Galeries Lafayette (all Paris), Wertheim (Berlin), Harrods and Selfridge's (London), Wanamaker's (Philadelphia), Macy's (New York), and Carson

9 *Commercial Art*, June 1927. Noting the American influence in Liverpool, the journal explained that the Bon Marché had to create an "atmosphere of gaiety and well-being". It also had its own art gallery.

10 'Art Nouveau' was the name of a shop established in Paris by Samuel Bing, 1895.

11 *Royal Academy Notes*, 1854. The painting hangs in The Tate Gallery, London.

Pirie Scott and Marshall Field (both Chicago). In the 1920s a Bon Marché opened in Liverpool. Unrelated to the Paris store: its customers were "fed, entertained and enlightened",[9] the proprietors, to use Zola's expression, being dedicated to 'Ladies Delight'.

Of these the most important is La Samaritaine since it confirms the suspicion, first excited by Eiffel's association both with the 1867 Exposition *and* with the Bon Marché, that the pioneering department stores were leaders of taste. The architect of La Samaritaine was Frantz Jourdain, a correspondent of Zola's who supplied him with the detail for *Au Bonheur des Dames*. Jourdain was an extraordinary man who founded the Salon d'Automne, birthplace of Fauvism. For his design of the La Samaritaine he was, again, inspired by an exhibition, this time the Paris Exposition of 1889, itself somewhat in the tradition of Paxton's Crystal Palace. At the time when Jourdain was actually designing La Samaritaine, he was also head of decorative arts for the Exposition of 1900, the international show which canonized Art Nouveau, a decorative style which was, with perfect symmetry, born in a shop.[10]

While the new department stores were evolving in Paris, the British found perversely anti-consumerist means of reconciling commerce with culture. British distaste for mass production was famously memorialised in John Ruskin's attack on Holman Hunt's painting, *The Awakening Conscience* (1853) where the critic says that you can tell the hero of the picture is depraved because the of 'fatal newness' and the 'terrible lustre' of the furniture.[11] The rise of the store and the museum created a demand for more information about furniture, but in Britain's case...old furniture.

Much taken by Ruskin's attack on new furniture, William Morris began to manufacture his 'traditional Sussex' chairs in the 1860s, but so strong was the 'antiques' movement in Britain that many of the trade journals regarded Morris furniture as fake. Yet, Morris' Arts and Crafts Movement was an ingenious means of reconciling Victorian historicism with Victorian materialism. Observing that "the growing preponderance of great stores is inimical to excellence of workmanship", and that "the services of the middleman are dearly bought at the price of artistic freedom".

The silversmith W. A. S. Benson neatly described the dogma of the Arts and Crafts Exhibition Society, a collaborative venture which in 1888 put on its first exhibition in The New Gallery. Benson, who deplored the alienation of maker from consumer and detested industrialized processes and machine finishes, was eloquent of a cultural conviction which has bedevilled British commerce ever since. But it is not insignificant that the reactionary movement of Morris, Benson and others had its origins in that then most modern of institutions: the exhibition.

Aristide Boucicaut's innovation in creating a vast, sophisticated store had sufficient richness and depth to sustain development in other countries throughout the twentieth century. When American emigré Gordon Selfridge opened his famous Oxford Street store in 1909 and used bombastic classical architecture to terrific effect, he was advertising a business which, to use Zola's words, was intended to 'create the poetry of modern activity'. In Germany, Berlin's Wertheim store in the Leipziger Platz was decorated with sculpture and bronze reliefs, marble and silver-plated terracotta; it had a carpet department panelled in Italian walnut and internal courtyards with decorative fountains. This too was in a sumptuous tradition established in Paris. Similarly in Italy, when Aldo Borletti's La Rinascente stores created the 'Compasso d'oro' award in 1954, making the shop into a design school, they were doing no more than continue a tradition of edifying the consumer which Boucicaut had begun almost a century before.

The crucial break with the Bon Marché tradition only came after the Second World War when the 'mall' was established. The *locus classicus* is the Lijnbaan in

57, 58 and 60. The catalogue, which began with Thomas Chippendale (1754), records a designer or a manufacturer's range, while stimulating consumer demand. Josiah Wedgwood opened a catalogue showroom, bringing supply and demand – commerce and culture – into nice equilibrium.

59. Owen Jones' Osler's gallery (1858) was a shop which imitated the form of the Great Exhibition (1851).

THE
GENTLEMAN
AND
CABINET-MAKER's
DIRECTOR.
BEING A LARGE
COLLECTION
OF THE MOST
Elegant and Useful Designs of Houshold Furniture
IN THE
GOTHIC, CHINESE and MODERN TASTE:

Including a great VARIETY of

BOOK-CASES for LIBRARIES or Private Rooms. COMMODES, LIBRARY and WRITING-TABLES, BUROES, BREAKFAST-TABLES, DRESSING and CHINA-TABLES, CHINA-CASES, HANGING-SHELVES, TEA-CHESTS, TRAYS, FIRE-SCREENS, CHAIRS, SETTEES, SOPHA's, BEDS, PRESSES and CLOATHS-CHESTS, PIER-GLASS SCONCES, SLAB FRAMES, BRACKETS, CANDLE-STANDS, CLOCK-CASES, FRETS,

AND OTHER
ORNAMENTS.
TO WHICH IS PREFIXED,
A Short EXPLANATION of the Five ORDERS of ARCHITECTURE,
and RULES of PERSPECTIVE;
WITH
Proper DIRECTIONS for executing the most difficult Pieces, the Mouldings being exhibited at large, and the Dimensions of each DESIGN specified :
THE WHOLE COMPREHENDED IN
One Hundred and Sixty COPPER-PLATES, neatly Engraved,
Calculated to improve and refine the present TASTE, and suited to the Fancy and Circumstances of Persons in all Degrees of Life.

Dulcique animos novitate trahit. OVID.
Ludentis speciem dabit & torquebitur. HOR.

BY
THOMAS CHIPPENDALE,
Of St. MARTIN's-LANE, CABINET-MAKER.
THE SECOND EDITION.
LONDON,

57

59

58

60

61. Asprey's Bond Street, London. By the mid nineteenth century, the availability of large sheets of glass changed the form of the shop.

61

62

62. Aristide Boucicaut's Bon Marché, Paris (1869-72) was the first department store, creating new standards of organisation and display.

63. An imaginary design by Karl-Friedrich Schinkel for a *Kaufhaus* ('store') of the 1820s is fascinatingly close to the Altes Museum which he built in Berlin (1823-30).

64, 65. The idea of categorising and displaying merchandise unites the museum and the store. Harrods in the 1920s.

63

64

65

66

67

66. La Samaritaine (1906), the Paris store which developed the language of exhibition design. Its architect, Frantz Jourdain, provided Emile Zola with notes for *Au Bonheur des Dames*.

67. Holman Hunt, *The Awakening Conscience* (1853). Tate Gallery, London.

68. Gordon Selfridge's swaggering London store (begun 1908) and the later malls turned shopping into culture.

68

69, 70. The high-minded Arts and Crafts Movement was launched in a shop and the 'exhibition', whether in a museum or a store, is central to consumer experience. William Morris' 'Sussex' chair was reviled by purists as a fake.

·ARTS·&·CRAFTS· ·EXHIBITION·SOCIETY· ·&· CATALOGVE ·OF·THE· ·FIRST·EXHIBITION·

·THE·NEW·GALLERY· ·121·REGENT·ST· 1888

69

70

71. Rotterdam's Lijnbaan (1951-53). One of the earliest pedestrianized shopping malls.

71

Rotterdam, by Johannes Hendrik van den Broek and Jacob B. Bakema. Built between 1951 and 1953 the Lijnbaan is a classic of the Modern Movement, but more significant in this context is the architectural design which separated the shop from the street, preparing the consumer for an experience separate from traffic.[13]

What Aristide Boucicaut did with exhibitions and concerts, malls now do with landscaping and themeparking. As early as 1928 the journal *Commercial Art* was publishing articles looking at the influence of modernist painting and architecture on shop design, illustrating mannequins set in pseudo-Cubist windows. Shopping maybe theatre,[14] but it is also art: Chicago's new Bloomingdale's has each floor inspired by an original building by Frank Lloyd Wright. The ground floor, the Imperial Hotel, Tokyo, followed by Unity Temple, the Arizona Biltmore, Oak Park, Falling Water and the Robie House.

It seems extraordinary that the relationship of commerce and culture was once considered antagonistic...

[13] The Lijnbaan is presently being remodelled by Derek Walker Associates. Having fallen into shabby disrepair, it is being redesigned to "lure shoppers...as well as tourists".

[14] W. F. Haug says "The salesroom is designed as a stage, purpose-built to convey entertainment", in *Critique of Commodity Aesthetics, 1986*.

72 – 74. The entrance to the Bon Marché, to say nothing of its size and scale, inspired Zola to describe stores as 'cathedrals of commerce'.

72

73

75

75. Furniture on the shop floor in the Bon Marché. The department store helped develop the idea of speculative consumption.

74

52

AU BONHEUR DES DAMES

Emile Zola

Zola (1840-1902) was one of the greatest French realist novelists. This extract from *Au Bonheur des Dames* is taken from April Fitzlyon's translation of 1957. The novel is in the series Zola called 'Histoire Naturelle et Sociale d'une Famille sous le Second Empire' and tells the story of Denise (an orphan from the provinces) and Octave Mouret (an entrepreneur), two very different characters involved with the rise of a revolutionary enterprise: the department store. Zola describes a new class and a new age, his vivid, detailed descriptions capturing the excitement of a new type of institution which, like a museum, made the produce of the world available to the public.

Denise had come on foot from Saint-Lazare station where, after a night spent on the hard bench of a third-class carriage, she and her two brothers had been set down by a train from Cherbourg. She was holding Pepé's hand, and Jean was following her; they were all three aching from the journey, scared and lost in the midst of the vast city of Paris. Noses in the air, they were looking at the houses, and at each cross-road they asked the way to the rue de la Michodière where their uncle Baudu lived. But, just as she was finally emerging into the Place Gaillon, the girl stopped short in surprise.

'Oh!' she said, 'just have a look at that, Jean!' And there they stood, huddled together, all in black, wearing out their father's old mourning clothes. She, an under-developed twenty-year-old, was carrying a light parcel, while on her other side, her small brother of five was hanging on her arm; her big brother, in the full flower of his magnificent sixteen years, stood looking over her shoulder, his arms dangling.

'Well!' she resumed, after a silence. 'There's a shop for you!' There was at the corner of the rue de la Michodière and the rue Neuve-Saint-Augustin, a drapery-shop, the windows of which, on that mild pale October day, were bursting with bright colours. The clock at Saint-Roch was striking eight, only those Parisians who were early risers were about, workers hurrying to their offices, and housewives hurrying to the shops. Two shop-assistants, standing on a double ladder outside the door, had just finished hanging up some woollen material, while in the shop window in the rue Neuve-Saint-Augustin another shop-assistant, on hand and knees and with his back turned to them, was daintily folding a piece of blue silk. The shop, as yet void of customers and in which the staff had only just arrived, was buzzing inside like a beehive waking up.

The high door, which cut off the corner of the Place Gaillon, was all of glass, surrounded by intricate decorations loaded with gilding, and reached to the mezzanine floor. Two allegorical figures, two laughing women, their bare bosoms exposed, were unrolling an inscription: AU BONHEUR DES DAMES. And the shop windows continued beyond, skirting the rue de la Michodière and the rue Neuve-Saint-Augustin where, apart from the corner house, they occupied four other houses which had recently been bought and converted, two on the left and two on the right. Seen in perspective, with the show windows on the ground floor and the plate-glass mezzanine floor windows, behind which all the internal life of the departments was visible, it seemed to her to be an endless vista. Upstairs a girl in a silk dress was sharpening a pencil, while near her two other girls were unfolding some velvet coats.

But Denise remained absorbed in front of the display at the main door. There, outside in the street, on the pavement itself, was a cascade of cheap goods, the bait at the entrance, bargains which stopped passers-by. It all fell from above: pieces of woollen material and bunting. Merino, cheviot cloth, flannels, were falling from the mezzanine floor, floating like flags, with their neutral tones — slate-grey, navy blue, olive-green — broken up by the white cards of the price tickets. To the side, framing the threshold, strips of fur were likewise hanging, straight bands for dress trimmings, the fine ash of squirrel, the pure snow of swansdown, imitation ermine and imitation marten made of rabbit. And below this, on shelves and tables, surrounded by a pile of remnants, there was a profusion of knitted goods being sold for a song, gloves and knitted woollen scarves, hooded capes, cardigans, a regular winter display of variegated colours, mottled, striped, with bleeding stains of red. Denise saw a tartan material at forty-five centimes, strips of American mink at one franc, and mittens at twenty-five centimes. It was a giant fairground spread of hawker's wares, as if the shop were bursting and throwing its surplus into the street.

A carriage forced all three of them to leave the centre of the square; mechanically they went along the rue Neuve-Saint-Augustin, past the shop windows, stopping again in front of each fresh display. First they were attracted by a complicated arrangement: above, umbrellas, placed obliquely, seemed to be forming the roof of some rustic hut; below, suspended from rods and displaying the rounded outline of calves of the leg, there were silk stockings, some strewn with bunches of roses, others of every hue — black net, red with embroidered clocks, flesh-coloured ones with a satiny texture which had the softness of a blonde woman's skin; lastly, on the backcloth of the shelves, gloves were symmetrically distributed, their fingers elongated, their palms tapering like those of a Byzantine virgin, with the stiff and seemingly adolescent grace of womens' clothes which have never been worn. But the last window, above all, held their attention. A display of silks, satins and velvets was blossoming out there, in a supple and shimmering range of the most delicate flower tones; at the summit were the velvets, of deepest black, and as white as curds and whey; lower down were the satins, pinks and blues with bright folds gradually fading into infinitely tender pallors; further down still were the silks, all the colours of the rainbow, pieces of silk rolled up into shells, folded as if round a drawn-in waist, brought to life by the knowing hands of the shop-assistants; and, between each motive, between each coloured phrase of the display, there ran a discreet accompaniment, a delicate gathered strand of cream-coloured foulard. And there, in colossal heaps at either end, were the two silks for which the shop held exclusive rights, the Paris-Bonheur and the Cuir-d'or, exceptional wares which were to revolutionize the drapery trade.

And so, from eight o'clock on the Bonheur des Dames, in all the glory of its great sale of winter fashions, was blazing in rays of bright sunshine. Flags were waving at the door, woollen goods were flapping in the fresh morning air, enlivening the Place Gaillon with the hubbub of a fairground; and the windows facing the two streets were displaying symphonies of window-dressing, the brilliant shades of which were further heightened by the translucence of the glass. It was an orgy of colours, the joy of the street bursting out there, the whole corner was a sumptuous spread, openly displayed on which everyone could go and feast his eyes.

But at that time of day, only local inhabitants, above all the small tradesmen, roused by such a display of streamers and plumes, were forming groups in doorways and at street-corners, their noses in the air, and making plenty of sour comments. Their indignation was aroused by the fact that in the rue de la Michodière outside the dispatch office there stood one of the four vehicles which Mouret had just launched on Paris: vehicles painted green, picked out with yellow and red, and with highly-varnished panels which flashed gold and purple in the sunlight. The vehicle which was standing there with its new and gaudy colour scheme with the name of the shop blazoned on its front and back and topped in addition by a placard bearing an announcement of the day's sale, when it had been filled with parcels left over from the day before it finally went off at the trot, pulled by a superb horse. Baudu, standing livid on the threshold of Le Vieil Elbeuf, watched it bowling along as far as the boulevard, carrying the hated name of the Bonheur des Dames all over the town, surrounded by a star-like radiance.

Meanwhile, a few cabs were arriving and lining up. Each time a customer appeared there was a stir among the page-boys lined up beneath the high porch, dressed in a livery consisting of a grey coat and trousers, and yellow and red striped waistcoat. Jouve, the shop-walker, a retired captain, was there too, in frock-coat and white tie, wearing his medal like a token of integrity of long standing, receiving the ladies with an air of solemn politeness, and leaning towards them to show them the way to the departments. Then they would disappear into the entrance-hall which had been changed into an oriental hall.

No sooner had they passed the door than they were greeted with a surprise, a marvel which enraptured them all. It had been Mouret's idea. He had recently been the first to buy in the Levant, at very favourable terms, a collection of antique and modern carpets, of rare carpets such as until then had only been sold by antique dealers at very high prices; and he was going to flood the market with them, he was letting them go almost at cost price, was simply using them as a splendid setting which would attract art connoisseurs to his shop.

On Monday, March 14th, the Bonheur des Dames was inaugurating its new building by a grand display of summer fashions, which was to last for three days.

From six o'clock onwards, Mouret was there, giving his final orders. In the centre, on a straight line from the main entrance, a broad gallery ran from one end of the shop to the other, flanked on the right and left by two narrower galleries, the Monsigny Gallery and the Michodière Gallery. The courtyards had been glazed in and transformed into halls; and iron staircases rose from the ground floor, iron bridges had been thrown across from one end to the other on both floors. It so happened that the architect was intelligent, a young man in love with modernity, and he had made use of stone only for the basements and the corner pillars, and then had made the whole of the rest of the framework of iron, with columns holding up the assembly of girders and beams. The counter-arches of the flooring and the internal partitions were of brick. Everywhere space and light had been gained, air was freely let in, the public had plenty of room to move about beneath the audacious curves of the wide-spaced trusses. It was the cathedral of modern business, strong and yet light, built for a multitude of customers. After the bargains by the door in the central gallery on the ground floor, there came the tie, glove and silk departments; the Monsigny Gallery was occupied by the household linen and the printed cotton goods, the Michodière Gallery by the haberdashery, hosiery, cloth and woollen departments. Then, on the first floor, there were the ready-made clothes, lingerie, shawls, lace and other new departments, while the bedding, carpet and furnishing materials, all the bulky goods and those which were difficult to handle, were relegated to the second floor. By this time there were altogether thirty-nine departments and eighteen hundred employees, of which two hundred were women. A whole world was springing up there amidst the life echoing beneath the high metal naves.

Mouret's sole passion was the conquest of Woman. He wanted her to be queen in his shop, he had built this temple for her in order to hold her at his mercy there. His main tactics consisted in intoxicating her with flattering attentions, trading on her desires, and exploiting her effervescence. Therefore he racked his brains night and day in search of new, bright ideas. Already, wishing to eliminate the fatigue of stairs for delicate ladies, he had had two lifts, upholstered in velvet, installed. Next, he had just opened a buffet, where fruit juices and biscuits were served free of charge, and a reading-room, a colossal gallery excessively richly and luxuriously decorated, in which he even ventured to hold picture exhibitions. But his subtlest idea was, when dealing with women devoid of coquetry, that of conquering the mother through the child; he let no force go untapped, speculated upon every kind of feeling, created departments for little boys and girls, stopped the mothers on their way past by offering pictures and balloons to their babies. This free gift of a balloon to each customer who bought something was a stroke of genius; they were red balloons, made of fine Indian rubber and with the name of the shop written on them in big letters; when held on the end of a string they travelled through the air, parading a living advertisement through the streets!

Publicity was, above all, a tremendous force. Mouret spent as much as three hundred thousand francs a year on catalogues, advertisements and posters. For his sale of summer fashions he had sent out two hundred thousand catalogues, of which fifty thousand, translated into all languages, were sent abroad. Now he had them illustrated with drawings, and even enclosed samples with them, glued on to the pages. His displays were bursting out everywhere, the Bonheur des Dames was staring the whole world in the face, invading walls, newspapers, and even the curtains of theatres.

But it was in the interior decoration of shops that Mouret revealed himself as a master without rival. He laid it down as a law that not a corner of the Bonheur des Dames was to remain unfrequented; everywhere he insisted upon noise, crowds, life; for life, he would say, attracts life, gives birth and multiplies. He put this law into practice in a variety of different ways. First of all there should be a crush at the entrance, it should seem to people in the street as if there was a riot in the shop; and he procured this crush by putting remnants in the entrance, shelves and baskets overflowing with articles at very low prices, so that working class people accumulated, barring the threshold, and gave the impression that the shop was bursting with people, when often it was only half full. Then, all through the galleries, he had the art of hiding the departments which were standing idle − the shawl department in summer and the cotton materials in winter, for example; he would surround them with active departments, drowning them in a hubbub. He was the only one so far to think of putting the carpet and furniture departments on the second floor, for in those departments customers were more rare, and the presence of them on the ground floor would have created cold, empty gaps. If he could have found a way of making the streets run right through his shop, he would have done so.

THE BON MARCHÉ
Georges d'Avenel

d'Avenel (1855-1939) was an economist and historian. His many books include *Le Français de mon Temps* (1905) and *Decouvertes d'Histoire Sociale, 1200-1910* (1910). This essay on the Bon Marché, one of the first 'scientific' accounts of a department store, is taken from his earlier book, *Le Mécanisme de la Vie Moderne* (1896).

Commercial freedom under Napoleon I encouraged the drapery stores of the present day, or rather, the precursors of those we see today; for not one of the innovative drapers who were so prosperous in the days when the actor Brunet played the part of 'M. Calicot' (a draper's assistant), not one of those companies famous in 1817, with names like the 'Fille mal Gardee', the 'Diable Boiteux', the 'Masque de Fer' or the 'Deux Magots', has survived. Many of those which replaced them during the reign of Louis-Philippe, such as the Belle Fermière and the Chaussee d'Antin, themselves subsequently floundered, or, like the Coin de Rue and the Pauvre Diable, went shamefully into liquidation.

Although department stores were successful, there were many losers. Even at the beginning of the Second Empire they still seemed so uncertain that the father of M. Deschamps, on being requested by his son, who had just founded the Ville de Paris, to entrust his savings to him, retorted with typical Lower-Norman suspiciousness: "I wouldn't put a hundred sous into a drapery store". M. Deschamps nevertheless went on to make a fortune which then seemed exceptional.

The Calicot mocked by Restoration caricaturists for daring, as a humble civilian, to sport moustaches and thus take on a military air, would no longer recognise themselves in their successors working for today's department stores, who may well be sportsmen or owners of hunting grounds which they rent out at exorbitant prices.

The new aristocracy is simply the product of intelligence and hard work. Its founders were people of modest means; capital played little or sometimes no part at all in the success of their enterprises. Aristide Boucicaut, the son of a modest hatter in Belleme (Orne), was employed at the 'Petit-Saint-Thomas' when in 1852, at the age of forty-two he became the partner of M. Vidau, the owner of a shop called Bon Marché at the end of the rue du Bac. There was nothing in the rather impecunious clientele, the seedy area and the turnover of only 450,000 francs to suggest the future development of the establishment. It has been claimed that Boucicaut gave away needles and thread to workers in the district in order to attract custom. The truth is that he was one of the first businessmen to have the idea of selling at very small profits.

Until this time the public had had the choice between good quality fabrics, which were expensive, and those which were cheap but of poor quality; the novelty consisted in selling guaranteed goods at the same price as shoddy goods. Another bold innovation was the use of fixed prices, which did away with the bargaining as well as with the vente au procede, *whereby the price of the object varied according to the appearance of the buyer; other elements of the organisation which Bouicaut, Heriot and their imitators vied with each other to perfect were the* rendu *('return'), which allowed the client to cancel a purchase at will, and lastly, the system of paying employees almost entirely by commissions on sales. Their efforts were crowned with success, although this was initially in terms of sales rather than profits.*

78

78. The left bank of Paris, site of Aristide Boucicaut's real Bon Marché and Emile Zola's fictional *Au Bonheur des Dames* (1883).

79. Aristide Boucicaut (1810-77), the provincial shopkeeper who created the modern store.

The genius of the creators of these vast counters lay precisely in that, although they all wanted to become wealthy, they aimed rather to sell in great quantity than to take much in profit, so that they virtually renounced any immediate gains in order to be all the more certain of future profits. One of the measures employed by the system was advertising, which could only give lasting results if the client was satisfied; and although the revolution which took place in the manufacture and price of fabrics some forty years ago was clearly to the advantage of the drapery trade, Parisians would not have found their way to a shop situated between the Petits Menages (a lunatic asylum) and the Hospital for Incurables without being led by a well-founded concern for economy. Thus, while sales at the Bon Marché rose from 450,000 francs in 1852 to 7 million in 1863, profits do not seem to have followed the same ascending curve.

In 1869, M. Boucicaut, having gradually bought up the whole area contained within the rue de Sèvres, the rue Velpeau, the rue du Bac and the rue de Babylone, laid the first stone of the industrial buildings which were to replace the houses previously converted ad hoc for commercial purposes. Sales had then reached 21 million francs. Having seen the turnover reach 67 million in 1877, the founder of this magnificent institution died without being able to follow its progress to its apogée. His son died soon after and his widow became sole heiress of the enterprise.

Left without close family on the threshold of old age and in possession of an almost 'royal' fortune – as people used to say in the days when kings were the richest of men – Marguarite Guerin, who had been an ordinary worker, could have sold the business profitably, knowing that it would not be continued by her own family, and retired. She did not give it a thought. She in turn wished to take on one of the noblest roles given to a proprietor in the commercial arena. Each partner in this historic couple had their share of greatness: the husband had put his conception of the new trade into effect with an exceptionally successful company; the wife, by means of contracts which were more like donations than sales, partly during her lifetime and partly after her death, transferred the company to the anonymous workers who had contributed to its success. She completed this task, whose social consequences went well beyond the limits of philanthropy, by endowing the phalanstery of the Bon Marché with retirement institutions and saving banks which are still models.

The success of the company had been unaffected by the death of M. Boucicaut; since the death of his widow in 1887 it has continued to develop uninterrupted. In 1893 turnover reached 150 million francs, the highest ever achieved by any company in the world.

80

80. Nineteenth-century
museums started
reproducing works of art in
their cast courts. Intended
for instruction, they
undermined the idea of
unique value in
masterpieces.

81. Some of the surplus
from the Great Exhibition
went into Marlborough
House and moved on to
other premises which
eventually became the
Victoria and Albert
Museum.

MUSEUMS

The department store and the museum arose out of the same circumstances, but since the consumer society which gave rise to them also promoted the notion that culture was remote from the market-place, they were in opposition, even while they had so much in common. As the department stores were huge edifices dedicated to the gods of commerce, so the museums were huge edifices in the service of nationalized culture. Each was in its different way dedicated to exhibition and it is noteworthy that both the great stores and the great museums were all located in the centres of great cities.[1]

1 It is equally significant that the other great institutions, created out of the same social circumstances, were the prisons and penitentiaries. These, of course, were dedicated to confinement, rather than display.

While department stores depended on the notion of *reproducibility*, the new museums sustained notions of traditional quality, of originality. The decision of the South Kensington Museum to introduce its public and students to exotic works of sculpture and architectural ornament reproduced in the form of casts was a fascinating diversion which did not really alter the assumptions about quality which underpined the notion of a museum. While casts of the Porta de la Gloria or the Gattamelata, on Cromwell Road or Fifth Avenue, posed questions subversive to connoisseurs, they did not undermine traditional notions of art because – in an age of moral certainties – the aesthetic qualities of the original were rarely questioned.

It is perhaps not surprising that given their concerns with legislating about taste, the museums attempted to impose aesthetic standards on the anarchy of the market-place. But the first museums had a limited conception of the public, and a limited respect for the public's standards of behaviour and capacity for independent judgement: the British Museum, for instance, was not prepared to accept unrestricted public access to its collections, special constables being recruited to help keep public order in the face of great art, hence the astonishing success of the Great Exhibition of 1851 which – uniquely – forged commerce and culture into a single event.[2]

2 The influence of the Great Exhibition was such that during 1851, attendance at the British Museum tripled.

Although it would be facile to attribute so vast and important an event as the Great Exhibition to autonomous acts of creative will by two mere individuals, it is not a perversion of the truth to say that is was nevertheless very much the inevitable outcome of events and initiatives set in train by Prince Albert, Henry Cole and their colleagues. Both Albert and Cole had the missionary zeal and the abundance of energy characteristic of born reformers.

Cole's own practical interest in commerce and culture began with designs for beer mugs and tea services in response to a Society of Arts competition of 1845. Ever the pedant, Cole had even consulted Greek vases in the British Museum to inspire him over details of the handles and, ever the opportunist, production of his designs in 1847 by the Minton Company led to the creation of a short-lived cooperative called Summerley's Art Manufactures. Soon after, in 1849, Cole started a campaigning *Journal of Design and Manufactures*, much of whose energy was spent on criticising the Government's Schools of Design. It was Cole's idea that art education should be in the service of industrial and commercial needs.

Enthused by these practical experiences of designing for industry, and encouraged by the popular success of smaller exhibitions organised under the auspices of the Society of Arts, a national enterprise whose ambitions and scale were appropriate to the leading industrial and military power on Earth was started by the Prince and the mandarin.

The Great Exhibition was so much a metaphor of national concerns that it is a study worthy of even more monographs than it has already caused and its details need not concern us here, but it is sufficient to suggest its scale and success by pointing out that with more than six million visitors paying entrance fees up to £3.00, the Great Exhibition had more than covered its costs. Clearly, there was a public appetite for displays of merchandise.

At the end of 1851 the Board of Trade commissioned Henry Cole, Richard Redgrave, A. W. N. Pugin and Owen Jones,[3] to spend £5000 of the profits on acquiring certain manufactured goods useful for future study, by students, the public and industry. One reason for this was that the Exhibition was held to have shown in an unfavourable light the achievements − or rather, lack of them − of the Government Schools of Design, established for more than fourteen years and so roundly condemned by the over-active Cole.

In his *First Report of the Department of Practical Art* Henry Cole had already encouraged the creation of Museums, which he strongly felt should be instructional: sauntering curiosity was not to be encouraged; on the contrary, Cole wanted to elevate the idea, perhaps on his own experience as a student in the British Museum, from being "a mere unintelligible lounge for idlers into an impressive schoolroom for everyone".

This is what the £5000 of manufactured goods bought from the Great Exhibition led to. The curious collection was installed in 1852 in a Museum of Manufactures in Marlborough House, Pall Mall. In turn, and in different locations, this became the Museum of Ornamental Art, the South Kensington Museum and, eventually, in 1899, the Victoria and Albert Museum.[4]

At Marlborough House the first room became an experiment in museology applied to the stuff of shopkeepers. Here Cole isolated and stigmatized certain merchandise which departed from the standards of excellence ordained by the Department of Practical Art. These standards, with a nice and characteristic confusion of the moral with the beautiful, expected 'common sense' to be more manifest in certain decorative flourishes than in others. This first room in Marlborough House became known as 'The Chamber of Horrors' and in it Henry Cole issued warnings about 'false principles' in design as chillingly certain in their dogmatism as a Victorian preacher's strictures to a fallen women might have been on the benefits of family life.[5]

On scrutiny, the *Catalogue of the Museum of Ornamental Art* reveals something of the structure hiding beneath Cole's blustering exterior: horrified by illiterate reproductions of bastardized historical detail by Birmingham manufacturers, Cole's theory was that ornament should be related to function and to form and to the material. His museum existed not to praise, but to evaluate, thus providing the critical apparatus denied these consumers in the competing display of the big stores. Cole respected the public's capacity to make judgements and simply wanted to provide his visitors with a means of making them. He writes in the Catalogue:

> "The public...are requested not to look at the articles in the Museum as mere objects, of *vertu*...but to examine their beauties or defects with reference to the principles laid down, to aid which examination critical notices will be found..."

By the time he retired in 1873 Henry Cole could look back on a career which had realised the Great Exhibition, turned the limp Schools of Design into a more vigorous national network of art schools and had made the South Kensington Museum "a storehouse for circulating objects of Science and Art throughout the Kingdom". His views were pioneering and modern, believing that museums should be critical and

[3] Richard Redgrave was a painter; A. W. N. Pugin was architect, with Charles Barry, of the Houses of Parliament and Owen Jones was an architect best remembered as author of *The Grammar of Ornament*, 1856.

[4] Legislation of 1850 had already provided for the creation of provincial museums. There followed: Birmingham (1867), Liverpool (1877), Leicester (1885), and Leeds (1888). In the United States, between 1870 and 1880, New York, Boston, Philadelphia and Cincinnati all acquired museums of their own.

[5] Charles Dickens, who knew something of family life, parodied Cole in his journal, *Household Words* which published an article called 'A House Full of Horrors' in 1852. In his novel, *Hard Times* (1854), Dickens has a character, clearly inspired by Cole, lecturing school children on carpet design.

evaluative, that industry and commerce were the modern muses and that the public, given sufficient stimulus was more than capable of making sophisticated choices of its own.

To Cole, the whole world was potentially a classroom, but there were considerable forces of reaction, not least in his own museum. While Cole's conviction about the unity of commerce and culture led him to encourage reproductions (provided they were of sufficiently high quality), some of his colleagues were dismayed at a low church attitude which threatened to rob prestige from art and donate it to the public. After his retirement, to the relief of many of the Keepers, including J. C. Robinson, who damned industrially manufactured metalwork as "mere unsaleable plate", the primacy of the past over the present was established and, instead of being an institution determined to coordinate commerce and culture for the benefit of each, the South Kensington Museum changed course for an antiquarian policy which remains in place today.[6] Meanwhile, the reforming role passed elsewhere.

Middle-class fear motivated a great deal of Victorian philanthropy. The other side of the coin to Samuel Smiles,[7] carried a menacing illustration on the 'there-but-for-fortune' theme. Thomas Coglan Horsfall was a prosperous Mancunian, imbued with the Ruskinian spirit of decent labour and very concerned that unless the proletariat could be educated to appreciate middle-class taste (and in so doing presumably acquire middle-class values), then they would be a threat as much as an embarrassment.

Horsfall's proposal for a Manchester Art Museum was first described in a letter to The *Guardian*.[8] By 1886 Horsfall's Museum was finally established in Ancoats Hall with the support of Ruskin and Morris. This was no ordinary museum, but an early exercise in outreach. But while Cole had wanted, at least in his Chamber of Horrors, to teach lessons about the modern world by derision, Horsfall aimed to teach by example. Moreover, Horsfall was suspicious of the brocades and other fancy stuffs of South Kensington, believing that the honest working man would react more favourably to that which was closest to his own experience.

The Museum contained mostly reproductions of works of art, in all the contemporary print media, as well as casts and mass-produced merchandise. An engraving of Holman Hunt's *Triumph of the Innocents* was set in a frame made by Ashbee's Guild of Handicrafts adorned with a quotation from Ruskin. The spirit of educational zeal suffused the enterprise,[9] and no more so in the part of the Museum that was both an image and reflection of the Chamber of Horrors. This was Horsfall's Model Cottage. Here W. A. Benson and William Morris filled a schematic sitting room and bedroom with furniture and fittings whose simple designs were intended for copying by the more diligent and ingenious model artisans. The rationale of the model cottage was explained by Horsfall:

"In respect of value as a means of cultivating taste...pictures are...far inferior to many of the products of the industrial arts."[10]

The idea that to learn to discriminate about a cup, a jug or a chair was revolutionary and certainly went far beyond Ruskin's idea of satisfying the spiritual needs of the artisan. It even went beyond Henry Cole's (an advance that Horsfall frequently emphasized). That part of Horsfall's intention was to undermine the status quo and short-circuit the tradesman,[11] puts him at the beginning of a radical tradition which led to the various offical design movements of the next century...both the cultural and the commercial ones.

In the United States the established museums were more conservative than in Britain, perhaps understandably so for a culture which depended on invention rather

[6] One interesting episode is characteristic. When in 1900 the Museum acquired from Samuel Bing's shop some Art Nouveau fittings, by Georges de Feure, for a suite of bedroom furniture, there was an outcry. The Advisory Council said the designs would corrupt students and the Press damned them as "shameful" and "vulgar".

[7] Author of *Self Help*, 1859.

[8] In February, 1877. Ruskin noticed the letter and repaid the compliment by commenting on it in the 1877 edition of *Fors Clavigera*.

[9] Horsfall's own publications included *What to Look for in Pictures* (1887) and *Suggestions for a Guide Book to Life*.

[10] In *Transactions of the National Association for the Advancement of Art and its Application to Industry*, 1888.

[11] And this, understandably, put him at odds with the trade, whose journals criticised the quality of Morris's furniture.

82

82. Henry Cole (1808-82)
came to public notice with
the design of a teaset whose
acclaim inspired him to
reform British commerce
and culture.

83

84

83, 84. Henry Cole was the
moving force behind the
Great Exhibition, a
metaphor of Victorian
preoccupations with trade
and morals.

85

86

87

85, 86. In Marlborough
House (first room, above:
fourth room, centre) Cole
organised a 'Chamber of
Horrors', denouncing those
manufacturers whose
products displayed 'false
principles'.

87. Henry Cole's reforms
were reflected in the
Manchester Art Museum,
where Thomas Horsfall
created a model workman's
cottage fitted out by William
Morris and W. A. S. Benson.

than tradition. When in 1912 John Cotton Dana of the Newark Museum organised an exhibition about the German Werkbund, New York's Metropolitan Museum declared it would have nothing to do with anything so crassly commercial. Commerce was not to cross this particular cultural threshold.

But by 1917 a change had occurred and the Metropolitan was organising an exhibition called *The Designer and the Museum*.[12] The following year the Museum hired Richard F. Bach, a journalist from *Good Furniture* magazine, as 'Associate in Industrial Relations'. In this curious post Bach began to organise an influential series of exhibitions which brought the idea of the artisan's model cottage to mid-town Manhattan.[13]

In 1919 a catalogue of a Bach show declared that it was a "demonstration of the practical or trade value of an art museum, a proof of the educational use made of museum objects for the advantage and improvement of current design". By the eleventh show in 1929, Bach had been given a department of his own and had distinguished architects, including Eliel Saarinen, Raymond Hood, Ely Jacques Kahn and Joseph Urban working with him. This show, entitled *The Architect and the Industrial Arts* was intended to run for six weeks and in the end ran to seven months.

Bach knew that in the modern world the Museum could provide laboratory material for practising designers. He mixed his metaphors and explained:

"They are literally working this mine and refining the ore to their modern purposes...These men have discovered that in the varied fields of industrial art production today, as of old, design is the final basis of comparison and the driving spur of competition."

These were momentous ideas, requiring a larger public than even the Metropolitan Museum could provide. In 1927 Macy's, New York's largest department store, put on its own exhibition. Partly funded by the Metropolitan Museum, the *Art in Trade Exposition* was a lesson in contemporary design for the store's huge clientele. The significance of a museum promoting trade and a department store exhibiting modern decorative art is clear: arising out of similar circumstances in the 1850s, but developing separately, by the 1920s the most sophisticated museums and the most ambitious stores realised the same thing, that commerce *is* culture. In the twentieth century the whole world has become a classroom. The question still left to debate is 'exactly what is to be the lesson?'

[12] It is interestingly revealing of national preoccupations that in the typescript catalogue of the exhibition, the lenders are named rather than the designers.

[13] See Essay #13

MUSEUMS AND THE INDUSTRIAL WORLD

Richard. F. Bach

In 1918 Bach left the School of Architecture at Columbia University to become Associate in Industrial Relations at New York's Metropolitan Museum where, at exactly the same time that Raymond Loewy and others established the profession of design consultant, he organised pioneering exhibitions on design. Bach made the Metropolitan the first museum to take twentieth-century industrial design seriously.

Museums today are active educational institutions, instruments of public service. The museum of art maintained for preservation and exhibition alone is an anomaly, out of tune with the aggressive spirit of practical usefulness which characterizes our time. It now searches out its quarry, diversifies its activities to meet demands of many types of people, and constantly seeks new avenues leading to yet other fields where the principle of art may do its missionary service. The avenues are as many as there are distinct kinds of energy and activity which require the aid or inspiration, the satisfaction or sustenance, offered by art. As the collection of books of not many years ago has become the working public library as we know it now, so the collection of rare objects of art is gradually assuming its proper place in public estimation as an influential educational agency. It is our privilege to predict that within another ten years our present slogan of "make the galleries work" will have taken its place among the foregone conclusions of museum thinking.

Yet while educational service, as a recognized and indispensable factor in museum work, is now on the fair road to final establishment, even in the smallest collections, such activity has as a rule been restricted primarily to cultural channels, whether developed within museum walls in the form of lectures or instructor service of varied kinds, or outside the walls in cooperative arrangements with public and other institutions. There is in addition the boundless unconquered territory of the art industries or lines of manufacture and production requiring artistic design as their chief element of value, yet counting upon machinery of the most modern type to bring their output within reach of the average purse — whatever that is in this changing time. In the industrial arts and in the types of thought which guide or control them, which serve or contribute to them, there is fertile virgin soil for the museum of art, offering direct as well as subtle lines of influence by which, properly used, museums may bind themselves forever to the most intimate feelings of the people, reaching them through their home furnishings, their utensils, their objects of personal adornment, their clothing.

The term art industries as here used must, however, be construed in its widest significance, being inclusive of the whole range of production from the extreme of the manual craftsman to the other pole of the items of cheap jewellery and ribbons, pasteboard boxes and wrappers, stock chairs, cotton frocks, or apartment house lighting fixtures. For the whole ground of the arts represented, for the whole range of producers, whether making but one piece of a kind or ten thousand from one good model, whether using but two machines or twenty-two in the process of bringing the object to the home, and whether making that object in two routine processes or one hundred and two, the museum has a definite value of resource and inspiration.

The highest service the museum can give to these many art industries lies in the

89

90

New York's Metropolitan
Museum became interested
in industrial design in 1917
and put on a succession of
exhibitions which rivalled
department stores.

89. The *Exhibition of
Industrial Design* (1922)
top.

90. *Modern Decorative Art*
(1926) centre.

91. *Fifth exhibition of work
by Manufacturers* (1920-21)
bottom, featuring products
by Colgate.

91

*maintenance of a standard of design. The museum must in a sense go into trade –
nothing less. It means that the museum must learn the difficulties as well as the
processes of manufacture, the vagaries of distribution and selling, the long, uphill road
of the designer, the problems of a manufacturer born with a conscience and daily
stultifying it in the sordid pursuit of coddling prospects, and those of the dealer who was
born without a conscience and finds that business is not worth the name without that
essential element; it means that the museum must reach artist and artisan alike, the
craftsman who gives the key and the quantity producer whose lathes and looms hum
the burden. And physically it means that the museum must maintain unlimited
facilities for study, depending upon a watch-like precision in the coordination of
departments within its own structure, practical lectures and guidance, and a field agent
who beards these lions in their dens, making a first-hand contact in factories and shop
and designing rooms. The initial equipment of splendid collections remain, of course,
the chief facility, but exploitation of the collections is an educational demand which
can no longer be put off.*

*But as we regard them now our art museums are museums of fine arts only; they
house the works of masters, each piece practically a law unto itself – the element of
mass production as foreign to its maker as radio-telephony. Or again, our art museums
have assumed the role of community centres, reaching the many, introducing a leaven
to the citizenry as a group. There is in neither of these the final solution for the needs of
the industrial world of our great producing centres. The industrial arts service of a fine
arts museum must, in the present economy of such institutions, remain but a sub-
department. The real solution lies in the industrial arts museums, the distinct
institution, separate plant and collection, affiliated with the fine arts museum by all
means but working as a unit in itself, under the same governing board, perhaps, but
with its own director and staff.*

*The museum of art of the future will be conceived in twofold purpose and significance
for the progress of our great communities. It will have two branches, a fine arts museum
in the present accepted sense and an industrial arts museum, devoted immediately to
the producing and merchandising fields, the two disposed architecturally, of course, in
order to profit as far as possible by the same machinery of utilities as well as of
administration, and certainly appearing as one before the public.*

*What will this industrial arts museum offer? To begin with, it will make no effort to
maintain collections of fine arts; for these examples of the great work of all times the
fine arts museum will serve as its source, administrative lines and conveniences being
arranged to make objects as readily accessible for study as conditions will permit and to
provide the easiest possible connections for the staff of the industrial arts museum.*

*On the other side, the industrial arts museum will be called upon to illustrate
processes of manufacture, machinery of production, something of the science involved in
the various fields touched, even raw materials and structural models being shown.
Where no other commercial exhibitions or like facilities exist it might be called upon to
play something of this role, while, in turn, it could undoubtedly count on natural history
museums, botanical gardens, and the like for illustrative material to supplement its
own collections.*

*There would be in such a museum replicas and even spurious pieces, their design
value being the only gauge of their usefulness; there would be intentional copies,
measured duplicates, embodying the closest study of the difficulties of craftsmanship of
other days in terms of the design forms in which those days indelibly wrote their story.*

*There would be in the industrial arts museum workrooms and laboratories, places
with proper light for looms, for colour work, for printing and so on, power for driving all*

types of modern machinery, individual workshops for craftsman, studios for designers, classrooms, a practical library - it being remembered that all of these facilities would be for study purposes only. Finally, there would be maintained a staff of experts familiar with the various aspects of most of the great fields of endeavour represented in furnishings, clothing, advertising, design of packages, jewellery, and the host of other decorative arts for which the American public expends a billion dollars a year. These experts will be men and women acquainted not only with the methods of design and manufacture of commodities in the industrial arts world, but also with the devious requirements of the enormous and intricate selling machinery of the country. There are in America a million stores selling various kinds of industrial art objects and other types of merchandise in which design is a direct or accessory selling factor, not including printing of newspapers and other publications. It is safe to say that in these myriad stores not a baker's dozen are manned by persons who have any other knowledge of design than the most superficial selling argument would require.

And, further, the work of the industrial arts museum would include a series of direct lines of influence and a group of cooperative arrangements or affiliations serving first, to bring always new materials to the museum and, second, to make lines of manufacture requiring artistic design always more willing to count upon the service and the good will of the museum. There would be maintained intimate relationships with the various trade organizations in both the producing and the selling fields, the national and local associations of manufacturers in many lines, the bodies of distributors, the societies of designers and craftsmen. There would be maintained a working cooperation with industrial arts and vocational schools (let us hope we shall soon have numbers of such schools to cooperate with!). There would be maintained, finally, working arrangements with other museums to the end that joint exhibitions might be offered, each institution bearing its share in contributing exhibits to establish the chain of production from the sample of wood to the library table, from the cocoon to the evening gown. For this purpose an assigned space would need to be accounted for in the plan of the industrial arts museum; a similar disposition being made to provide for galleries in which to show collections of modern products, selected by a collaborative jury from the museums and the trades, some of these collections being constant, as a record of our time, others being temporary and synchronized with the markets or seasons in various lines of production. This space, like the preceding, would need to be separately accessible from the street. These exhibitions, furthermore, would be made to have telling effect toward public education by explanatory lectures, worked out, if possible, by coordinating museum work with the curicula of the public schools.

The whole programme as suggested seems an egregious one for a single institution to undertake. To be sure, the entire compass of the plan would fall to the lot of only a few large museums in leading cities. For the institution in the smaller community the plan would require modification to bring the service of the industrial arts museum into accord with the leading products of the locality: pottery for Trenton, furniture for Grand Rapids, textiles for Philadelphia, and so on.

One may even visualize an industrial arts school as a factor of the industrial arts museum, separately operated, to be sure, but closely affiliated for purposes of demonstration.

But this is all a shot into the future. Until long-headed business men and far-sighted museum administrators see the value and purpose of the industrial arts museum, the fine arts museum will be called upon to maintain an industrial arts service for manufacturers and designers, craftsmen and dealers, approximating the work of an industrial arts museum as far as its own character and equipment will permit. Some of

our leading institutions have made efforts in this direction. At the Metropolitan Museum of Art this work has been gradually built up, the patient effort entering into it having been rewarded in the establishment of a separate section of industrial arts, now in its ninth year. This work has become extensive and varied in a manner to prevent description in the compass of these pages. Suffice it to say that the interest is widespread among producers in numerous industrial art lines, that they use the collections religiously as a source of inspiration, that they work faithfully and in always greater numbers in every field from cretonne to soap wrappers, from millinery to vacuum bottles, and that the exhibition of current work by manufacturers and designers has become a regular feature in the season's programme. And further, that there are now maintained during the busy season regular sessions in the nature of study-hours, which are diligently attended by buyers and salespeople anxious to learn at first hand the principles of good design. But these are only the merest beginnings for a community the size of New York. Whole continents remain to be explored in this direction.

Yet we venture to say that the industrial arts museum will be a logical feature in the life of America in the future; that such museums will receive consideration at the same time or even sooner than fine arts museums in municipalities which are primarily industrial centres; that the use of the museum as a laboratory, as an adjunct of the factory and workroom, and as a resource for the designing room will be as well understood and as regularly practiced as are the present accepted functions of our fine arts museum.

92. The Design Museum, London (1989).

URBANISM

Museums and stores, with their shared commitment to exhibition and their common locations in city centres, are the characteristic institutions of nineteenth-century industrial culture. Our own century has created institutions and urban forms of its own.

The way things are made is changing and as a consequence, so is what they *mean*. This applies to products as well as to entire cities. Not only are technological innovations altering the processes of manufacture and construction, but new financial environments are transforming the established relationship of client-designer-manufactuer-customer.

For years Western manufacturers held huge stocks, until the Japanese taught them *Kan ban*.[1] Phased product planning, a means of controlling the manufacturing process, was perfected during the United States space programme in the sixties, but Japanese manufacturers have taught that multi-disciplinary teams work better. Hitherto distinct, the four stages of product-planning, design, manufacture and marketing all now overlap. So that in some cases marketing begins before manufacture, or even, exceptionally, before a design is finalised. The decision to implement any particular design is deliberately delayed, so as to sustain an atmosphere of creativity and choice.[2]

Nowhere is this more obvious than in city buildings. From the Chicago Tribune competition of 1922, where Adolf Loos' design for a monumental Doric column was only one of a number of surprising entrants, architects realised a new form of expressive power in the commercial environment. The history of twentieth-century architecture could be written as a history of twentieth-century commerce as much as twentieth-century culture. In 1928 New York's Chrysler Building had a pinnacle recalling a car's radiator mascot; Lever House (1950-52) was green and clean, as one would expect of the headquarters of a detergent company; Seagram in 1958 was sober and sombre; Transamerica Tower in 1969 projected the 'dynamic' image of a west coast conglomerate; Pennzoil Place in Houston in 1973 and Citicorp Building in New York of 1974 opened competitive stakes in assertive skylines; the AT&T (1978) building projected the bogus probity of a monopoly about to be dismembered and, back in Houston, the Transco Tower of 1982 established a style christened '*High Corp*' as glittering, sleek and meretricious as this year's company report.

Historically, architecture has always provided a model (as well as a metaphor) for design. Building as advertising prefigured the phenomenon of the designer cult. As the most ancient design discipline, the transformations facing architects and architecture is full of clues about the future for other design disciplines. There is anxiety among architects that, so far from being the hallowed professionals responsible for the mother of the arts, those asethete-technicians who, like Palladio, know both divine proportion and how to mend a leaking roof, their role in the face of momentous technological and economic change is being reduced to a 'design subcontractor'. More facade tinkerers with a bit part in the joke that ends 'Your building's alright, but the architecture's been blown off.'[3]

There is now a phenomenon known as fast-track construction. The very name is suggestive of new influences in the world of architecture and urban design. The techniques of fast-track construction have changed the relationship between architect and client. While once the chairman of a large company doing well would have

[1]   *Kan ban* is usually translated as 'just-in-time', the method of inventory control used by Japanese manufacturers who call up components from suppliers only when they are actually needed, thus eliminating the expensive need to carry stock. Of course, this system imposes disciplines which, by spotlighting bottle-necks, force efficiencies throughout the process. To work well, *Kan ban* requires different levels of subcontractors who, by developing special skills in limited areas, can be called on to contribute to the product development process.

[2]   The jargon term is 'variety reduction', always left until last.

[3]   See Essay # 15

commissioned a headquarters to confer prestige on his business, and would have spent time discussing the concept and the details with his architect, nowadays major buildings are more likely to be have been bought by property developers sensitive to plot ratios, rentals and gross margins rather than the niceties of egg and dart mouldings or the refinements of Attic classicism.

This change is not just a subtle adjustment in the patronage system, but evidence of something more fundamental in the way products — and, since they became advertising, buildings can often be spoken of in such terms — are called into existence. The absurdity of promoting a 'classical revival' is made all the more poignant in the face of systematic changes in the creative process which, at their worst, threaten to rob architects of any responsibility other than the selection of colour, texture and the decoration of surface.

Just as in the latest forms of new product development, with all the hitherto distinct stages of the process now being simultaneous, some buildings are rising above the earth's surface with their 'design' as yet unfinished. Frankly, we could have buildings without architects, because more often than not, the actual building technology is in other people's hands. Driven by the fearsome imperatives of interest rates, commercial developments are often built *before* they are designed. Neat refinements in the process make construction as slick as the production of Model T Fords used to be. First the piling, then the steelwork, then the metal decking for the floors, then...architecture. Other forms of technology have further debased architecture: with their predetermined life of often no more than thirty years, with their cavernous provision of data cabling and their bristling spines of microwave antennae, for many big companies the new headquarters is not so much an opportunity to flirt with the mother of the arts as "a part of the telecommunications budget."[4]

4   According to Frank Duffy of London architects, DEGW.

These new buildings form a part of an environment that is being transformed. In America, 'suburban downtowns' have been scenes of astonishing growth.[5] These are new perimeter centres built, mostly, to serve the service industries and are, poetically, both symptom and cause of an historical decline in blue-collar work experienced everywhere in the industrialised West. The suburban downtowns feature buildings as — not so much advertising — as packaging, designed to be seen almost subliminally as you drive past at 55 or 70 m.p.h., making detail and scale irrelevant. Telecommunications means these buildings don't have to be in city centres. Air travel means they don't have to be near railways. In fact, they can be anywhere, neat system-built packages of the enterprise economies.

5   Memorably described by Mark Swenarton, *Building Design* 17th June, 1988.

And the only focus of the suburban downtown is...the shopping centre, or mall. Here among the knowledge-based service industries you find culture. The United States has more than 30,000 shopping malls, employing nearly 9 million people. They are used by 169 million consumers every month, spending nearly $600 billion every year.

The great architect, Louis Kahn, said that "Los Angeles is truth, whether you like it or not."[6] In the past decade Houston has displaced Los Angeles as a vision of the city of the future. Here you have what Ada Louise Huxtable called "an act of real estate, rather than an act of God or man."[7] Here is a version of contemporary truth. Houston, which has grown without constraints of geography or planning, whose urban form was determined by the ubiquity of the private car, is a city with no centre to speak of except...the Post Oak Galleria.[8] Where once a city centre — downtown — might have contained municipal buildings, museums, public spaces and a major railway terminus, Houston has a 420,000 square foot shopping mall, with Tiffany, Neiman-Marcus and other prestige shops humming prosperously under coruscating

6   *California Environment* (exh. cat., Los Angeles County Museum of Art, 1976).

7   In *The New York Times* 13th February, 1976.

8   The choice of 'Galleria' for shopping centre is revealing to the student of commerce and culture. Gallery became a synonym for museum after antique sculptures were first displayed in the Galleria of the Vatican.

93

94

95

96

In the United States major commercial buildings have always been a form of corporate advertising.

93. The Chrysler Building (1928) is like a car mascot...

94. AT&T (1978) gave itself spurious 'tradition' with a Chippendale pediment...

95. The purity of soap is suggested by Lever House (1950-52)...

96. ...and the overwhelming might of a major bank by the clarity and precision of the Citicorp Building (1974).

97, 98. The architecture of America's 'suburban downtowns' is temporary townscape, designed to be seen at 55 m.p.h.

99. Laying the foundations for the tallest building in London (Canary Wharf). New methods of construction allow buildings to be erected before the 'design' is finished.

99

97

98

101

100

Shopping malls extend the department store into small cities.

100. The interior of Houston Galleria.

101, 102. Trammell Crow's malls: 'The Commons Deerbrook', Houston and 'El Mercado', Miami.

102

chandeliers dependent from a glass barrel vault.

Post Oak Galleria was the work of developer, Gerald Hines. Another developer making a significant contribution to Houston is Trammell Crow, a company which, since it was founded in 1948, has been responsible for more than one hundred shopping malls. There is no particular Trammel Crow *style*, rather there is a response to the market-place. The crucial measure is *traffic count*.

Photographs in a recent Trammell Crow prospectus betray the chilling anomy of American urban life, with malls located at popular junctions in Houston's loose grid. These are pilgrimage centres for those located somewhere in the north east corner, between Wertheimer and Gessner. The hierarchy of form, image and detail is instructive. Some historical claims are made for certain new malls, by attaching folksy identifiers such as 'commons' or, if in Florida, by building a mall in mission church style. Upper scale malls are indicated by flag poles, more ambitious planting and luxury finishes, polished granite is typical, and are always shown in greater perspective in the developers' photographs.

These malls are among the most flamboyant construction projects in contemporary America. They are decorated sheds which are part museum, part church. Certainly, they are places where the solemn rituals of high consumption capitalism are carried out. Just like the *grands magasins* of nineteenth-century Paris, they offer the experience of speculative consumption. When shopping becomes a pastime and not a requirement for survival, when architecture becomes packaging, when 'designer' becomes a priest, there is a crisis in culture which vigorous commerce cannot completely disguise.

A generation ago Reyner Banham could write without irony of the thrilling experience of American urban life:

> "The Santa Monica/San Diego intersection is a work of art, both as a pattern on the map, as a monument against the sky, and as a kinetic experience as one sweeps through it."[9]

9 'Los Angeles: the Architecture of the Four Ecologies' in *California Environment* (exh. cat., Los Angeles County Museum of Art, 1976).

Urban architecture is now more concerned with packages than with monuments. At the same time, this gives prominence to the designer, but trivializes his work.

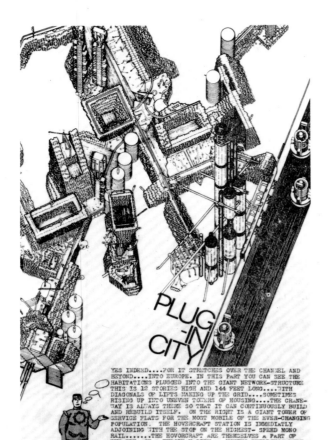

103. Archigram's 'Plug in City' (1964) reflects the confidence of young architects of the period.

104. Offices at Quinlan Terry's Richmond Riverside development.

105. Stuart Lipton's Broadgate office development, London, was built following American methods of management and construction.

103

104

106

105

106. The eighteenth-century style Adam's Committee Room in the Lloyds' Building was designed for committee members who felt that the powerful-but-conservative identity of Lloyds' had been lost in the new building.

107, 108. The Isle of Dogs left, and Canary Wharf right, will be developed without planning restrictions.

107

108

78

DE-SKILLED ARCHITECTURE

Peter Murray

Murray (*b*.1944) is a well-known architectural journalist and publisher. A one time editor of the *RIBA Journal*, he is now publisher of *Blueprint*, the successful magazine of topical architecture and design.

*T*wenty *years ago the architectural profession was at the height of its power; the post-war building boom was going full tilt, the Government depended on architects to boost the politically important house building statistics, architectural posts in local authorities were senior and high spending. Architects viewed the world on a macro scale – after all, they were designing whole new towns and demolishing and replacing city centres. Development was comprehensive; the topics of conversation were transportation, housing, building systems, regional and urban planning and, yes, world resources. Younger architects produced schemes of vast megalopoli stretching from Edinburgh to Paris; the Archigram Group's 'Plug in City', published in 1964'[1], had a brashness that made Le Corbusier's Ville Radieuse look like a conservation project.*

1 **Peter Cook Archigram, 1972.**

But despite their world view, their knighthoods and their peerages, the ingrained optimism and reforming zeal of the Modern Movement, architects had less influence on fundamental issues than they thought – as they now admit.

Today, as a response partly to public criticism and partly to changing patterns of work, the architect's sights are set on closer horizons; his conversations now are about marketing, style, community architecture, classicism and about facades. New methods of organisation in the development and construction of buildings, particularly in the fast moving commercial sector, threaten to turn the architect from prime consultant to exterior decorator.

The structural separation of the facade from the rest of the building has been standard practice in commercial buildings since the Victorians invented the steel frame, but the building was generally conceived as a whole; it is only in recent years that the two have become divorced aesthetically, the various parts frequently undertaken by different hands. This dislocation can be seen in refurbished buildings whether they are Victorian facades which are propped up and 'conserved' while a contemporary office-block is constructed within, or a sixties structure whose rational curtain walls are stripped off to be replaced by bright new poMo garments; it can also be found in new buildings of all manners and styles. The High-Tech Sainsbury's Homebase Store in Brentford, Middlesex, by Nicholas Grimshaw and Partners, displays a dramatic roof of elegant wings supported by tension cables from a tall steel mast, but despite the building's external promise, the interior is indistinguishable from any of the other tin sheds that conventionally house D. I. Y. emporia, the underside of the dramatic roof is camouflaged beneath an array of poorly arranged lights, signs and heating ducts.

Even the traditionally built Richmond Riverside development designed by Quinlan Terry is skin-thin. The classically inspired development, constructed of solid brickwork, lime mortar, stone mouldings and timber windows, sports an interior which bears no relationship to the nostalgic facades; the suspended ceilings and standard partitions clash painfully with the proportions and details of another age.

The proliferation of specialists involved in the design of a modern building – space planners, service, communications and retail consultants, interior designers, project managers, trade contractors have all affected the architect's role in the building team. It is said that Sir George Grenfell Baines, who in the post-war period built BDP into Britain's largest architectural practice, made a habit of arriving at meetings with clients and his other consultants five minutes late, just to remind them how indispensable the architect was to the proceedings. Today, they would probably start without him.

When a party of architects from Arup Associates, in anticipation of their commission to design the first phases of the Broadgate development, visited New York to learn about American methods of office building, they asked Kevin Roche of Roche Dinkeloo how he saw the architect's role in the design of speculative commercial architecture. "Like designing the wrapping on a chocolate bar" was the reply.

The size of new commercial developments, the speed with which they are built, the scale of the risk, the technology involved in their construction and in the services they contain, have redefined the organisation of the building team. When developers like Broadgate's Stuart Lipton were planning their revolutions in development construction they looked at the conventional, architect-led programme, and found it wanting. Borrowing much from American experience, they developed systems of professional project management in which the architect was just one of many consultants, working to plans developed by office layout specialists, to structures and methods developed by construction teams, and using details designed by specialist trade contractors.

"We are the new master builders", a member of Lipton's team once told me. Indeed, the methodology of the late twentieth-century builder/developer bears some comparison with his eighteenth-century counterpart.

"The master builder's technique was this;" writes Sir John Summerson "he would sign a building agreement with the ground landlord, preparatory to taking a building lease of perhaps sixty, perhaps ninety years, with a peppercorn rent for the first year or two. During this period he would erect the carcass of a house – simply a brick shell with floors and roof – and offer it for sale."[2] Not very different from the modern developer joining forces with a landowner, organising the design and erection of a building to 'shell and core' standard (wall, floors and a roof). Which a tenant will then complete himself. Other similarities include the employment of labour by subcontracting each of the skills to individual craftsmen, rather than using a contractor who employs a whole range of skills, a method of organisation that was first used by Thomas Cubitt in the early 1800s.

2 ***Georgian London***, 1962; p.78.

Despite the fact that the shell and the interior of the Georgian house might be carried out by a different hand to the exterior, there was a consistency of design that arose from a coherent contemporary taste, reinforced by craft skills and guidance in the form of pattern books like the Adam brothers' ubiquitous Works in Architecture. *For the modern master builder consistency is less easy. His office buildings must be flexible to allow for a variety of users, to be able to change from dealing rooms to professional suites at a drop of the FTSE index; they must appeal equally to a tenant from Tokyo or to a banker from Frankfurt. Its multitude of services channelling everything from effluent to data, cost more than the building structure.*

The modern office building is essentially a giant piece of equipment which must be able to adapt to its circumstances – if it cannot, its life is limited like the numerous sixties' blocks currently under deconstruction. If it can, it must also be able to accept new additions and designs. Richard Rogers's Lloyd's Building is the embodiment of the architecture of change – designed to last the organisation at least fifty years, in contrast to its more traditional previous buildings which forced the underwriters to move four times in fifty years because of their inability to cope with expansion. Despite the rigour and consistency with which Roger's architecture is carried through he argues that it is inclusive, that it can accept change and alternation carried out by others and maintain its quality.

The continual dilemma of the architect as to whether he is practising an art or providing a service – something that rarely troubles the design fraternity – has an added significance in the light of two contrasting trends. On the one hand there is the increasing public interest in architecture which, either by Royal example or mere national prejudice, veers more towards the traditional than the original, and on the other there is the demand for 'star' architects – who are ex-officio "strong ideas" men and who are by no means traditional – by developers, corporations and public bodies who, acting like latter day Medicis, sign up Stirling, Meier, Foster, Isozaki, Venturi et al, to produce buildings which are as much an expression of the architect's own cultural view as any painter's canvas is of his. These architects insist on calling the shots and are less prone to the de-skilling process already discussed.

The offshoot of the star system is the current trend for what the letting agents call "landmark buildings". The proliferation of styles – which critics describe disarmingly as pluralism – the endless choice of materials available to the contemporary architect, as well as the increasing number of cooks stirring the architectural pot, is fast creating an urban landscape of visual chaos. The Isle of Dogs Enterprise Zone – which is free from planning restrictions – is an example of what can go wrong when architects and developers are given a free hand. While individual buildings vary in architectural quality from the good to the diabolical, the whole is jarring and incoherent, a cacophony of High-Tech, Low-Tech, English Extremist and predictable Post Modern, of corrugated steel, stone, brick, of tall and squat.

It is enough to give credence to the Prince of Wales's idea of ten commandments for building. A set of rules which would protect scale but not determine style, restrict materials but not the way they were used and provide guidance on the relationship between buildings, streets and public spaces could perhaps bring a sense of order to the Post Modern city. Architects will no doubt cry "foul" and claim it to be a curb on their artistic freedom (although it could well relieve them from much of the petty fogging bureaucracy of planning control) – but they often produce better buildings under tight constraints. A period like the sixties when the architect's role was rarely criticised, was hardly a credit to the profession. Then he saw himself almost as a director, in theatrical terms, determining the way we would all live better lives.

Now he accepts what was the reality all along, that he is just the scene shifter.

110. New York's Museum of
Modern Art has a design
collection shown on the
basis of style alone,
suggesting that 'design' is
only superficial.

111, 112. When London's
Design Centre opened in
1956, it selected particular
merchandise – including
this Morphy Richards iron
– for special attention. This
was the origin of the
designer cult.

110

111

112

113. At the same time as the
Design Centre was created,
Italy's La Rinascente
department store began its
influential Compasso d'oro
awards which turned
designers into celebrities.
Rome's La Rinascente,
1957.

113

THE DESIGNER CULT

'Celebrity' according to novelist John Updike, 'is a mask that eats the face'. Thus, celebrating the 'designer' is not only a cruel parody of the design process (whose essence and strength is making the excellent commonplace), but a nasty assault on the person as well. The lionisation of design and the designer are historically parallel with the isolation of the fine artist and the banalisation of art in museums...to say nothing of the unstoppable development of the department store, now increased in acreage and impact in the form of the shopping mall.

The design cult, with all its pompous absurdities, travesties of value and its short-lived pretension, is a sort of revenge of tradition on the carefully nurtured culture of mass production.

But this was inevitable, given the coincidence of circumstances that nationalised culture in museums, put the world on display in stores, held 'design' to be the motor of trade and, later, valorised excessive consumption of frivolities with the cachet of *style, fashion* or *taste*.[1] Hitherto separate, these gauges of consumption were all rolled into the 'designer', one of the silliest (and most transient) manifestations of Post Modernism's dedication to expensive trash.

While soon after 1945 Italy had its *Ricostruzione*, Germany had its *Wirtschafts-wunder*, the Americans continued to build on established prosperity and Japan had its own economic miracle, Britain had the mixed economy welfare state. One curious characteristic of this localised example of the nationalisation of culture was that the Arts Council, founded immediately after the War, failed to recognise (or, rather, insisted on ignoring) the common appetites which stimulated desire for both goods and ideas.

In the world of the Arts Council, official culture was high art. It was also parochial high art. You could have 'Peter Grimes', but not Elvis; Henry Moore, but not a Chevrolet. But at the same time, the spokesmen for industrial design were having something of a hard time getting the rationale of this mass-produced aesthetic across to a nation which, excepting the tiny clientele of the Arts Council, was always treated as obdurately philistine.

If the opening of the Design Centre[2] in 1956 is seen in this context, then it is not surprising that some remarkable claims were being made for design. With anything industrial or commercial excluded by definition from the Arts Council's agenda, the Design Centre was not so much free as required to promote an aesthetic under the utilitarian disguise of trade. Thus, a somewhat queasy relationship between commerce and culture was established. In the mid nineteenth century there had been frequent discussion about the relationship of trade to morals; in the mid twentieth century, morality's dialogue was with trade.

The official view, circa 1956, was that design meant *good design* which is to say, a particular style admired by the educated officials. And the taste was as specific as the Arts Council's. The officals were both more sympathetic to Scandinavian culture than to American, Italian, German or Japanese. Behind the bright front of the Design Centre in its early years lurks the sombre ghost of Scandinavian trade propaganda,

[1] Thorstein Veblen's landmark study, *The Theory of the Leisure Class*, 1899, was the source of the useful coinage 'conspicuous consumption'. Veblen's ideas resurface in all discussions of consumer affairs. See, for instance, Essays #15 & #16.

[2] The Council for Art and Industry was set up in 1934 as a consequence of Lord Gorell's report which called for "a special building for exhibitions of industrial art". 'Art' was dropped from its title in 1944. It changed its name to the Design Council in 1960.

gussied-up and fortified into something altogether less invincible: the morally persuasive good design.

In his autobiography, Gordon Russell confirms the influence of Sweden:

> "I had been to Sweden where I acquired many friends...in the early 1920s...It was a most exciting interlude after the grim, dull war years and I was able to discuss many matters of mutual interest with Swedish designers."[3]

3 *A Designer's Trade*, 1968.

When the Design Centre opened, it was in a cultural commercial no man's land between art and industry. While New York's Museum of Modern Art had given the American public twenty years experience of venerating design and the designer, lionising everyday objects put the British on their guard. Gordon Russell found that manufacturers disliked any idea of control, retailers felt their own judgement was being challenged, while designers felt the Centre's selections were too timid. Shown in 1956 were a Russell-Hobbs kettle, a Morphy-Richards iron, an Adamsez lavatory basin and a Hille dining chair. The dominating aesthetic was bland, Anglo-Saxon modernity, with gentle radii designed not to shock.

Significantly, and revealing of the tastes, or at least of the preoccupations of the organisers, the exhibits mainly comprised flatware, ceramics, appliances and furniture, the sort of goods whose stable technology posed no real challenge for a designer other than that he should conform to a sort of genteel Euro-normality. Thus, while a particular suitcase had been severely criticised by the Consumer's Advisory Council and British Standards Institute, it was exhibited in the Design Centre because it matched official expectations about right and proper appearance. This early separation of form from function segregated 'design' as something both immanent and material, but actually rather separate from the manufacture or use of the product.

Contemporary press comment on the opening is revealing. The Design Centre was, according to the *The Times*, "window-shopping...on a hitherto unprecedented scale."[4] Walter Gropius, at this time a Professor of Architecture at Harvard and no longer Director of the Bauhaus, was among the first visitors. His comment conveys the limited power of the thousand or so exhibits to excite curiosity:

4 *The Times*, 23rd April 1956. Later, in a caustic article, Reyner Banham was to damn the Design Centre as 'Her Majesty's Fashion House', *New Statesman* 27th January, 1961.

> "I have rarely seen such well made display fittings in an exhibition of this character."[5]

5 *In Design* no. 89, 1956.

Such measured enthusiasm reveals that the ex-director of the Bauhaus was now more in tune with the excitement of American than the austerity of Europe. Yet, the Design Centre *was* intentionally more like a well-executed shop than a museum.[6] At exactly the same time a real Italian shop instituted its own design prize, almost as if to demonstrate that while in welfare state Britain popular aesthetics were to be handled by a bureaucracy remote, by its own admission, from industry, public and the professions, in Italy design was more commonplace, already the stuff of department stores.

6 The prejudices are revealed in a comment by W. J. Worboys, the Council's Chairman: "I would suggest that you should not think of the Design Centre as a museum: it is a live, active, moving thing.", *Design*, no. 89, 1956.

When La Rinascente conceived its 'Compasso d'oro' ('Golden Compass') award in 1954 it was as a worthy complement on the commercial front to the high-minded (but very often abstruse) activities of the Milan Triennale. It says something for the fecundity of Italian material culture that in 1954, 470 manufacturers submitted nearly 6000 objects.

One well-travelled English commentator said, "Elsewhere in Europe the destructiveness of twentieth-century commercialism was merely philistine; in Italy it became an ideal".

That the number of entries tended to decline over the years may be evidence of either the extent to which the Compasso d'oro successfully promoted the aesthetic of the judges, rendering the competition itself redundant, or may be evidence of the draconian standards of the judges (who, like the Council of Industrial Design) had a strict taste for formal simplicity.

Nevertheless, this was how many of the 'name' Italian designers became known. The stage army did not carry spears, but rather electronic and electrical appliances. By the mid sixties the number of prizes was slowly stabilising, reaching an average which matched the rhythm of Italian industrial production. In 1967, for instance, prizes were given to an emerging generation of celebrities: Rodolfo Bonetto (for the Olivetti 'Auctor' machine tool), to Vico Magistretti (for the Artemide 'Eclipse' lamp), to Marco Zanuso and Richard Sapper (for the Siemens 'Grillo' telephone, and to Joe Colombo (for the O-luce 'Spider' lamp). Although there were important differences between London's Design Centre and its awards and Milan's Rinascente with its Compasso d'oro (notably that design awards in London were usually given to distinguished individuals often working outside an established industrial system which resisted change, while in Italy they were more often than not actually a part of it), each is an example of the same phenomenon. Essentially European in its structure, what happened in Milan and London[7] was the isolation of particular merchandise for special attention. One way of achieving this was to revert to the idea of authorship.

In America, the same thing occurred but in a characteristically more free enterprise way. In 1953 an architect called Benjamin Thompson — a founding partner, with Walter Gropius, of The Architect's Collaborative, and Chairman of the Department of Architecture in the Harvard Graduate School of Design — set out to demonstrate in proper late Bauhaus fashion that 'art is everywhere', but particularly in his own shop. Design Research opened in Boston in 1953, bringing the inclusive ethic of the Bauhaus onto Main Street. Here Thompson built up a stable of designers, mostly European, including Marimekko (discovered at the 1958 Brussels World Fair), Kai Franck, Bruno Mathhson, Paul Kjaereholm and Joe Colombo, in pursuit of his notion that a modern shop should be as much about ideas as products. The local paper even compared it to New York's Museum of Modern Art.[8]

Contemporary accounts emphasise that the way it looked, the way it felt, the unusual quality of the merchandise, all made this commercial venture into a cultural experience. Paradoxically, for an individual who had wanted to get art out of museums, Benjamin Thompson had turned his shop into an art gallery. And just like the Museum of Modern Art, Design Research isolated individuals as the 'form givers' of the twentieth century; every assumption about the merchandise it sold was that each item was the consequence of individual, autonomous acts of creativity. Just like the Museum of Modern Art, Design Research proposed to the world a troupe or a retinue of identified names, of famous individuals responsible for the characteristic designs of the late twentieth century.

The Design Centre, the Compasso d'oro and Boston's Design Research were idealistic ventures, but by celebrating designers, they distorted and limited the idea of *design*. By lionising individuals, by emphasising the significance of design to business and by suggesting that one expression of form was at any given moment probably superior to another, these high-minded bodies have contributed to the contemporary 'designer cult'.

Robert Burchfield, editor of *The Oxford English Dictionary*, says the word 'designer' was first recorded in 1649, in that this is the earliest occurrence of the freemasonic trope that God is the great designer of the Universe. The present connotation is

[7] And in Brussels too. Here a 'Signe d'or' was instituted in the early sixties. The international jurists included Count Sigvard Bernadotte from Sweden, Paul Reilly from London and Raymond Loewy from Palm Springs.

[8] *Boston Sunday Globe*, 6th November 1966.

114

The idea that life and art
are inseparable goes back to
the Bauhaus and is a
fundamental of the Modern
Movement world view.

115

116

114–116. The most
impressive attempt to make
art and life into a successful
commercial venture
occurred in Boston in
1968, when Architect
Benjamin Thompson
created his Design Research
store. The store was like a
modern museum...where
everything was for sale.

117

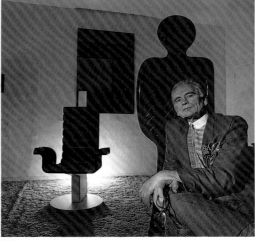

118

**119. It was a short step
from the celebration of
designers to the celebration
of brands. After Murjani
created 'designer' jeans with
Gloria Vanderbilt, and
Coca-Cola sportswear he
next intends to create Jeep
gear.**

Jeep.
Don't you just love being in one?

The Jeep image of dependability, durability, quality, and style intends to extend beyond the vehicle and on to products ranging from active sportswear to outdoor equipment.

Jeep brand
From tents to apparel, the potential to extend the Jeep brand name successfully into other product categories is enormous.

Consumer Research
Jeep scored greater than three times the average, and 92% higher than Murjani's next highest scoring brand concept.

Jeep brand sportswear and accessories
The initial Jeep gear product line will consist of sportswear and related accessories.

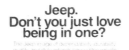

Jeep brand bicycles & sporting goods
The product line will be expanded to include non-apparel items over the next two years.

Jeep gear customers
Like the vehicle, the customers will be upscale adult men and women 25–45 years old.

Jeep gear
Paving the way with clothes for city action. Rugged, casual, comfortable. Designed to be durable and give you all the room you need to maneuver your way through the city. Jeep gear will become your second skin the second you put it on. It's the one-of-a-kind style statement in the tradition of the one-of-a-kind driving statement.

Jeep gear stores
Jeep gear will be available through better department stores, direct response catalogs and through freestanding Jeep gear stores.

Independently operated, Jeep gear stores are designed to appeal to the target audience. The stores feel comfortable, yet, will look new and innovative in a mall.

Jeep in America's shopping malls
The environment of the stores set off the Jeep brand clothes and other gear to their best advantage, and extends the presence of the Jeep brand name into America's shopping malls.

New and sophisticated
The Jeep gear stores are very "Jeep." They grew out of a new, sophisticated, urban approach to a traditional environment. The design uses muted earth tones and textured wall surfaces.

119

entirely contemporary (and usually pejorative) perhaps dating from no earlier than that moment in 1978 when Manhattan jeans entrepreneur, Mohan Murjani, persuaded Gloria Vanderbilt to have her bottom photographed wearing her signature trousers.

The pathology of the designer cult is most typically represented in the exploits of Pierre Cardin. Born it Italy in 1922, the son of displaced French parents, Cardin was a model, actor, and dancer in his youth, before drifting to Paris and into the atelier of a *couturier* in the Faubourg St Honore. Soon moving onto Schiaparelli, Lelong and Dior, by 1950 Cardin was employing his own seamstresses and by 1959, in a reference book event, he invented *prêt-à-porter*. This was his stroke of genius, turning hand-made *couture* into ready-to-wear merchandise.

At this stage Cardin believed that *'haute couture'* should serve the masses[9] an admirably populist sentiment, but one encouraged somewhat to excess by Cardin, who, after success with the *hommes à la mode* when his men's wear collection was launched in 1960, now licenses his name for chocolate and almost everything else, quite literally from soup to nuts. Indeed, Cardin has put about his designer name so much that the Academie Française is now considering the coinage of a new word...*Cardiniser*.[10]

Pierre Cardin is a corporation. With his $2.5bn. turnover, his frying pans, his *prêt-à-porter*, his expensive fragrance and his cheap hardware demonstrate the bizarre power of the 'designer'. His licensees may say that what they are buying is entry into a market without the expense of building up a brand, but the ugly truth is that what you have here is celebrity in league with high consumption capitalism.[11] The magic of the designer cult is rubbing off on the hapless consumer, and it is the spurious magic of celebrity itself.

The 'designer' cult is simply another device to stimulate trade, no different to the *good design* movement of the fifties and sixties. Murjani, for instance, having used-up Vanderbilt and made a success of Coca-Cola clothes, is now looking for other authoritative brands to validate his merchandise. The latest is Jeep, a 'concept' soon to be applied to tents, bikes and clothing, to be sold in stores with 'muted earth tones and textured wall surfaces'. With the Murjani Jeep range, the notion of celebrity passes from people to products.

The lionisation of brands is only a contemporary extension of the lionisation of individuals. But by the late eighties, the astonishing improvements in artificial intelligence and in reproduction technologies has, at least for the time being, tended to isolate and expose creative individuals so that this same 'designer' is now a fashionable poseur rather than an *eminence grise*. 'Designer' is a journalistic cliché, as robbed of meaning as 'executive', 'de luxe' or 'turbo'. Its currency a consequence of the contemporary preoccupation of making aesthetic choice a measure of social competition.

9 And had himself drummed out of the Chambre Syndicale de la Couture, Paris, for his apostasy.

10 According to *Apparel International*, June 1983.

11 *Forbes* estimated, in its edition for 2nd May, 1988; that Pierre Cardin had more than 800 licensees. By comparison, Dior had 300, Yves St Laurent 200 and Calvin Klein 12.

THE ARISTOCRACY OF CULTURE

Pierre Bourdieu

Bourdieu (*b.*1930) is a Professor of Sociology in the College de France. This essay is originally from his book, *Distinction*. Bourdieu's work on popular culture is comparable to his predecessor, Roland Barthes, and his contemporary, Jean Baudrillard. With them he shares a passion for explaining the everyday which — ironically — is baffling to all but a sophisticated elite of intellectuals. Still, the expenditure of so much academic effort on what was earlier considered trivial, is evidence of how seriously culture nowadays takes commerce.

Rarely does sociology more resemble social psychoanalysis than when it confronts an object like taste, one of the most vital stakes in the struggles fought in the field of the dominant class and the field of cultural production. This is not only because the judgement of taste *is the supreme manifestation of the* discernment *which, by reconciling reasons and sensibility, the pedant who understands without feeling and the man of the world who enjoys without understanding, defines the accomplished individual. Nor is it solely because every rule of propriety designates in advance the project of defining this indefinable essence as a clear manifestation of philistinism — whether it be the academic propriety which, from Riegl and Wölfflin to Elie Faure and Henri Focillon, and from the most scholastic commentators on the classics to the avant-garde semiologists, imposes a formalist reading of the work of art, or the upper class propriety which treats taste as one of the surest signs of true nobility and cannot conceive of referring taste to anything other than itself.*

Here the sociologist finds himself in the area par excellence *of the denial of the social. It is not sufficient to overcome the initial self-evident appearances, in other words to relate taste, the uncreated source of all 'creation', to the social conditions of which it is the product, knowing full well that the very same people who strive to repress the clear relation between taste and education, between culture as that which is cultivated and culture as the process of cultivating, will be amazed that anyone should expend so much effort in scientifically proving that self-evident fact. He must also question that relationship, which is only apparently self-explanatory, and unravel the paradox whereby the relationship with educational capital is just as strong in areas which the educational system does not teach. And he must do this without ever being able to appeal uncondition ally to the positivistic arbitration of what are called facts.*

Hidden behind the statistical relationships between educational capital or social origin and this or that type of knowledge or way of applying it, there are relationships between groups maintaining different, and even antagonistic, relations to culture, depending on the conditions in which they acquired their cultural capital and the markets in which they can derive most profit from it. But we have not yet finished with the self-evident. The question itself has to be questioned — in other words, the relation to culture which it tacitly *privileges — in order to establish whether a change in the content and form of the question would not be sufficient to transform the relationships observed. There is no way out of the game of culture; and one's only chance of objectifying the true nature of the game is to objectify as fully as possible the very operations which one is obliged to use in order to achieve that objectification.*

1. Well-tempered Clavier
Labourers
Household servants   3
Craftsmen, small shopkeepers   2
Clerks   1
Middle-level civil servants   4.5
Commercial middle management, secretaries   9
Technicians   10.5
Medical and social services   11
Primary schoolteachers   7.5
Cultural mediators, art craftsmen   12.5
Industrialists, commercial entrepreneurs   4
Upper civil servants   5
Private sector executives, engineers   14.5
The professions   15.5
Secondary schoolteachers   31.5
Teachers in higher education, producers of art   33.5

2. Rhapsody in Blue
Labourers   20.5
Household servants   3
Craftsmen, small shopkeepers   20
Clerks   22
Middle-level civil servants   27.5
Commercial middle management, secretaries   26.5
Technicians   42
Medical and social services   20
Primary schoolteachers   20
Cultural mediators, art craftsmen   22.5
Industrialists, commercial entrepreneurs   25.5
Upper civil servants   15.5
Private sector executives, engineers   29
The professions   19
Secondary schoolteachers   12.5
Teachers in higher education, producers of art   12

3. Blue Danube
Labourers   50.5
Household servants   35.5
Craftsmen, small shopkeepers   49
Clerks   52
Middle-level civil servants   34
Commercial middle management, secretaries   29.5
Technicians   21
Medical and social services   15.5
Primary schoolteachers   10
Cultural mediators, art craftsmen   12.5
Industrialists, commercial entrepreneurs
Private sector executives, engineers   18.5
The professions   15.5
Secondary schoolteachers   4
Teachers in higher education, producers of art

121. Pierre Bourdieu is fascinated by popular taste. These graphs analyse high, middle and low-brow preferences in music.

Paradoxically, the games of culture are protected against objectification by all the partial objectifications which the actors involved in the game perform on each other: scholarly critics cannot grasp the objective reality of society aesthetes without abandoning their grasp of the true nature of their own activity; and the same is true of the opponents. The same law of mutual lucidity and reflexive blindness governs the antagonism between 'intellectuals and bourgeois' (or their spokes-persons in the field of production). And even when bearing in mind the function which legitimate culture performs in class relations, one is still liable to be led into accepting one or the other of the self-interested representations of culture which 'intellectuals' and 'bourgeois' endlessly fling at each other. Up to now the sociology of the production and producers of culture has never escaped from the play of opposing images, in which 'right-wing intellectuals' and 'left-wing intellectuals' (as the current taxonomy puts it) subject their opponents and their strategies to an objectivist reduction which vested interests make that much easier. The objectification is always bound to remain partial, and therefore false, so long as it fails to include the point of view from which it speaks and so fails to construct the game as a whole.

Only at the level of the field of positions is it possible to grasp both the generic interests with the fact of taking part in the game and the specific interests attached to the different positions, and, through this, the form and content of the self-positionings in which these interests are expressed. Despite the aura of objectivity they like to assume, neither the 'sociology of the intellectuals', which is traditionally the business of 'right-wing intellectuals', nor the critique of 'right-wing thought', the traditional speciality of 'left-wing intellectuals', is anything more than a series of symbolic aggressions which take on additional force when they dress themselves up in the impeccable neutrality of science. They tacitly agree to leave hidden what is essential, namely the structure of objective positions which is the source, inter alia, of the view which the occupants of each position can have of the occupants of the other positions and which determines the specific form and force of each group's propensity to present and receive a group's partial truth as if it were a full account of the objective relations between the groups.

Our inquiry sought to determine how the cultivated dispositions and cultural competence that are revealed in the nature of the cultural goods consumed and in the way they are consumed vary accordingly to the category of agents and the area to which they applied, from the most legitimate areas such as painting or music to the most 'personal' ones such as clothing, furniture or cookery, and, within the legitimate domains, according to the markets − 'academic' and 'non-academic' − on which they may be placed. This led us to establish two basic facts: on the one hand, the very close relationship linking cultural practices to educational qualifications and, secondly, to social origin and, on the other hand, the fact that, at equivalent levels of educational capital, the weight of social origin in the practice − and preference − explaining system increases as one moves away from the most legitimate areas of culture.

The closer one moves towards the most legitimate areas, such as music or painting, and, within these areas, which can be set in a hierarchy according to their modal degree of legitimacy, towards certain genres or certain works, the more the differences in educational capital are associated with major differences both in knowledge and in preferences. The differences between classical music and modern songs are reproduced within each of these areas by differences (produced in accordance with the same principles) between genres, such as opera and operetta, or quartets and symphonies, periods, such as contemporary and classical, between composers and between works. Thus, among works of music, the 'Well-Tempered Clavier' and the 'Concerto for the Left Hand' (which, as we shall see, are distinguished by the modes of acquisition and consumption which they presuppose), are opposed to the Strauss waltzes and the Sabre

Dance, pieces which are devalued either by belonging to a lower genre ('light music') or by their popularization (since the dialectic of distinction and pretension designates as devalued 'middle-brow' art those legitimate works which become 'popularized') just as in the world of song, Brassens and Ferre are opposed to Guetary and Petula Clark, these differences corresponding in each case to differences in educational capital.

Thus, of all the objects offered for consumers' choice, there are none more classifying *than legitimate works of art, which, while distinctive in general, enable the production of distinctions ad infinitum by playing on divisions and subdivisions into genres, periods, styles, authors, etc. Within the universe of particular tastes which can be recreated by successive divisions, it is thus possible, still keeping to the major oppositions, to distinguish three zones which roughly correspond to educational levels and social classes (1)* legitimate taste *i.e. the taste for legitimate works, here represented by the 'Well-Tempered Clavier' (histogram no.1), the 'Art of Fugue' or the 'Concerto for the Left Hand', or, in painting, Brueghel or Goya, which the most self-assured can combine with the most legitimate of the arts in the process of legitimation — cinema, jazz or even the song (here, for example, Leo Ferre, Jacques Douai) — increases with educational level and is highest in those fractions of the dominant class that are richest in educational capital (2)* middle-brow *taste which bring together the minor works of the major arts, in this case 'Rhapsody in Blue' (histogram no.2), the 'Hungarian Rhapsody', or in painting, Utrillo, Buffet or even Renoir, and the major works of the minor arts, such as Jacques Brel and Gilbert Becaud in the art of song, is more common in the lower-middle classes than in the working classes or in the 'intellectual' fractions of the dominant class, (3) finally, 'popular' taste, represented here by the choice of works of so-called 'light' music or classical music devalued by popularization, such as the 'Blue Danube', 'La Traviata' or 'L'Arlesienne', and especially songs totally devoid of artistic ambition or pretension such as those of Mariano, Guetary or Petula Clark, is most frequent among the working classes and varies in inverse ratio to educational capital (which explains why it is rather more common among industrial and commercial employers or even senior executives than among primary teachers and cultural intermediaries).*

'Classical taste', Panofsky observes, 'demanded that private letters, legal speeches and the shields of heroes should be "artistic"...while modern taste demands that architecture and ash trays should be "functional" (Panofsky Meaning in the Visual Arts, *1955).*

But the apprehension and appreciation of the work also depend on the beholder's intention, which is itself a function of the conventional norms governing the relation to the work of art in a certain historical and social situation and also of the beholder's capacity to conform to those norms, i.e. his or her artistic training. To break out of this circle one only has to observe that the ideal of 'pure' perception of a work of art qua work of art is the product of the enunciation and systematization of the principles of specifically aesthetic legitimacy which accompany the constituting of a relatively autonomous artistic field. The aesthetic mode of perception in the 'pure' form which it has now assumed corresponds to a particular state of the mode of artistic production.

This demand is objectified in the art museum; there aesthetic disposition becomes an institution. Nothing more totally manifests and achieves the autonomizing of aesthetic activity vis-a-vis extra-aesthetic interests or functions than the art museum's juxtaposition of works. Though originally subordinated to quite different or even incompatible functions (crucifix and fetish, Pieta and still life), they tacitly demand attention to form rather than function, technique rather than theme, and, being constructed in styles that are mutually exclusive but all equally necessary, they are a practical challenge to the

expectation of realistic representation as defined by the arbitrary canons of a familiar aesthetic, and so lead naturally from stylistic
relativism to the neutralization of the very function of representation. Objects previously treated as collectors' curios or historical and ethnographic documents have acceded to the status of works of art, thereby materializing the omnipotence of the aesthetic gaze and making it difficult to ignore the fact that − if it is not to be merely an arbitrary and therefore suspect affirmation of this absolute power − artistic contemplation now has to include a degree of erudition which is liable to damage the illusion of immediate illumination which is an essential element of pure pleasure.

In short, never has more been demanded of the spectator, who is now required to reproduce the original operation whereby the artist (with the complicity of his whole intellectual field) produced this new fetish. But never perhaps has he been given so much in return. The naive exhibitionism of 'conspicuous consumption', which seeks distinction in the crude display of ill-mastered luxury, is nothing compared to the unique capacity of the pure gaze, a quasi-creative power which sets the aesthete from the common herd by a radical difference which seems to be inscribed in 'persons'.

122. The Coca-Cola story is one of management continuously exciting demand for this most superfluous of products. The original trademark was conceived in *c.*1887 by a book-keeper, Frank Robinson.

123. Four generations of the Kenwood mixer. By restyling the basic product, Kenwood created a new domestic market.

122

123

94

COMMODITY AESTHETICS

W. F. Haug

Haug (*b*.1926), founder of the journal *Das Argument*, is a Professor in the Free University of Berlin. In his book *Commodity Aesthetics*, from which this essay has been extracted, Haug provides a radical Marxist perspective on consumerism.

With increasing productivity, the problem of profit realization for the oligopolies returns in a new guise. Now the productive forces of organised private capital no longer impinge on competing rivals so much as on their boundaries, directly on the limits of the relations of production, which define the demands of society, in so far as these demands bring purchasing power to bear. In a society like the United States of America, a large part of the total demand depends on the need to replace a part of this stock of consumer durable goods as it wears out or is discarded. Since the way towards a total labour-saving society would amount to the abolition of capitalism, capital is now taking umbrage at the excessive durability of its products. One technique which answers this problem of in particularly longer-lasting consumer durables like cars, electrical appliances, light bulbs and textiles, is to reduce the quality of the products. This technique has radically altered the standards of use-value in many areas of private consumption in favour of a shorter lifetime and lower resistance to wear.

The technique of reducing a commodity's useful life has been discussed under the concept of 'artificial obsolescence', which has been translated by the expression 'product senility'. The commodities enter the world with a kind of timing device which will trigger off their inner self-destruction within a calculated period. Another technique is that of reducing the quantity being sold in an unaltered guise. A compromise between qualitative obsolescence and quantitative reduction of a product is shown in the way cloth is becoming thinner, etc. Commodities particularly suitable for quantitative reduction are foodstuffs and similar articles for private consumption which are sold in filled, brand-named packets.

When the price and styling of a carton of pasta, remain unchanged but the content is reduced, a new term in practical commodity selling appears – the concept of 'fill-level'. It describes the level to which the package is – just about – filled. The word appears specifically when the commodity's packet is regularly sold partially empty. Since the empty space, which makes the fill-level obvious, is open to conscious perception, certain firms have adopted the highly ingenious concealed device of a false bottom in the packaging.

As a rule, the reduction of use-value both in quality and quantity is compensated for by ornamentation. But even so, articles for use still last too long for capital's need for valorisation. The more radical technique seizes not only upon a product's objective use-value, in order to shorten its useful life in the sphere of consumption and generate further demand prematurely: this technique starts with the aesthetics of the commodity. By periodically redesigning a commodity's appearance, it reduces the use-lifetime of the specific commodity, whose models are already functioning in the sphere of consumption.

This technique, which we shall call aesthetic innovation, operates as follows: its full development and systematic application through the length and breadth of the commodity world, especially the sector for private consumption, requires the subordination of use-value to brand-name, thus in a sense ensuring the victory of the monopoly commodity, since every brand-name intends to set up an aesthetic monopoly. Nonetheless, aesthetic innovation, like other such techniques, is not historically speaking an invention of monopoly capitalism, but it emerges regularly wherever the economic function, which is at its root, arises.

In the eighteenth century...aesthetics innovation was already a quite consciously employed technique. A decree passed in 1755 for the cotton industry of Saxony reads that for the good of the 'factory' – which here still meant craftshops, as production was still organised according to distributing firms (commodities were produced by individual proprietors for the capitalist wholesaler) – it was necessary that apart from the finer garments, the commodities themselves should be made to a new taste and design.

Note that the point is not the benefit of the buyers, as would be the case from the stand-point of use-value; rather, it is for the benefit of the entrepreneur, i.e. from the stand-point of exchange-value which is concerned with regenerating demand. Even though aesthetic innovation was not invented by monopoly capitalism, it is only within this system that it achieves a crucial meaning, dominating production in all decisive branches of the consumer goods industry and playing a vital role in the capitalist organization of this industry. Never before was it manifested in such an aggressive manner. Like political slogans, posters in department-store windows announce the desires of capital, which command the customers, 'Out with the old in with the new!', for example, was a slogan recently used by a furniture chain.

The record company, Polydor issued an advertising poster for retailers with the message, "Old records are boring". A picture, produced with all the tricks of the trade, plainly functioned as 'instructions for use': it showed the ruin of the 'old' records bent, burnt, melted, broken. This is the pipe-dream of monopoly.

The buyers experience the aesthetic innovation as an inevitable, although fascinating, fate. In the aesthetic innovation the commodities are driven by an inner dynamism, and appear as 'things which transcend sensuousness'. What appears here, reflected in the modification of the commodity's skin and body, is the fetish character of the commodity in its monopolistic peculiarity. The illusion is maintained that it is the things as such which change by themselves. "Ties are getting broader and more colourful", writes a journalist in all seriousness. If this utterly superficial statement is out of place in the business section of a newspaper whose editors should know better, it still adequately reflects what the buyers and users experience. Ties appear, like skirts, shirts, trousers, shoes, furniture, etc. as part of the natura naturens *of the commodity world. The aesthetically differentiated generations of commodities replace one another, as if from natural causes, like changes in the weather. From the stand-point of the capitalists, the the process looks completely different. For them it belongs to the realm,* natura naturata, *of their capital, which it is their business to produce amid anxiety and high risk. They require that the social 'necessity' – for such is the use-value of their commodities – be sanctioned again and again to achieve the determining aim of the valorisation stand-point.*

CREATIVITY AND TECHNOLOGY

John Ruskin damned Henry Cole for his arranged marriage of art with industry. For Ruskin, art was more to do with morals than with trade. That Cole saw morality in a certain sort of formal perfection made little difference to Ruskin; he believed that mechanisation was dehumanising. The concept of design for production was quite beyond Ruskin's comprehension. Limited by his own experiences of industry as debased and brutalising, Ruskin passed on a grotesque inheritance to generations of Englishmen who were as unable as he to see quality as separate from rarity.

Ruskin was correct to suggest that mechanisation − or, indeed, any other technological change − altered the course of the creative process. What he neglected to consider was the benefits which this alteration might entail. Certainly, the first generation of machines usurped the craftsmen's role in shaping products, but they also augmented his ability to realise new ideas.

It was the interruption in the division of labour caused by machines which first made the role of the designer identifiable. As soon as it was identifiable, it could be quantified. As soon as it was quantified it could be valued. So far from debasing creativity, new technology made it possible to cost it.[1]

1 As early as 1840 the *Report of the Select Committee on Design* included manufacturers' estimates of the cost of design as a proportion of total production costs. At the time it was reckoned at not more than 1%.

The recognition of *the value of ideas* was a point in the progress of industrial civilisation at least as important as double entry book-keeping or mass production. As soon as the value of ideas is recognised, then they have to be protected. The first campaign to copyright textile patterns was launched in the 1830s.

The introduction of the rotary cotton printing machine allowed patterned fabrics to be mass produced in realistic volume for the first time.[2] Steam-power and the mechanical engraving of the patterns on the cylinders were further fillips to increased production which, leading to increased consumption, also created a demand for more new designs. At first, technical restrictions (in particular, problems of register) limited the scope for designers, and most were restricted to small floral patterns, dots or stripes which, with small repeats, were also attractive to garment manufacturers as waste was at acceptable levels.

2 The rotary printing machine was perfected by Thomas Bell and first used in Lancashire in 1785 by Livesey, Hargreaves, Hall & Co.

The protection of ideas, by patent, copyright or registered design, is an increasingly important and lucrative part of legal activity. This is the forensic counterpart to the observation, acknowledged as valid by many researchers, that the number and frequency of patent applications is a useful measure of *economic* activity in any given country.

To be patentable any product must be both new and capable of being produced industrially; more subjectively, it must exhibit a spirit of innovation. It is interesting that the law considers design as, by definition, superficial.[3] Patents protect the workings of any product for up to fifty years, but a registered design (defined legally as 'outward form') has only fifteen years protection. However, the law recognizes that *trademarks* have an indefinite life.

3 A White Paper called Intellectual Property and Innovation was published in April, 1986.

With the declining value of hardware, intellectual property − whether patents, registered designs, or trademarks − may in the long term be the most valuable asset which a company possesses. Edith Wharton recalled her mother saying:

"Never talk about money and think about it as little as possible."[4]

4 In her autobiography, *A Backward Glance*, 1934.

But modern designers and manufacturers are denied the felicity of this ultramontane attitude. Indeed, one of the characteristic features of industrialised economies at the end of the twentieth century is the amount of effort being put into (a) generating creative ideas and (b) wondering how they might be costed and sold. For certain, whatever Ruskin might have said, technology has not inhibited creativity, it has simply changed its character.[5]

5 See Essay #18.

The designer cult has its commercial equivalent in another global phenomenon, the valuation of brands. H. G. Wells recognised the importance of brands in that they short-circuit the retailer by speaking on the manufacturer's behalf directly to the consumer. Consumers assert their identity through their choice of brands, creating what the Librarian of Congress, Daniel Boorstin, has described as "consumption communities."[6]

6 In *The Decline of Radicalism: Reflections on America Today*, 1963.

Deregulation of financial markets has contributed to global movements of capital which in turn means that many businesses, hitherto considered invulnerable to predators, are often targets for acquisition. Since Wedgwood and the industrial revolution, design has been used to contribute to business, nowadays design still has a very specific role in business, but it is more concerned with imagery than with substance.

With consumer goods, brands are the heraldry. The global success of a product such as Coca-Cola demonstrates the extraordinary power that brands have to command loyalty and extend consumer expectations. Brand valuation brings to mind Goethe's definition of genius in that it 'gives form to the indeterminate'. More specifically, in a turbulent world economy, brand valuation, according to experts Interbrand, aims to "achieve consistent, objective methods of determining how much brands are worth to their owners."[7] As graphics are fundamental to the perception of a brand, this form of design has become of immense economic significance in the post-industrial economy.

7 Interbrand's actual method of valuating a brand is to take average earnings over three years and multiply them by a factor which reflects the extent of advertising support and the position in the market-place. This follows standard accounting principles for asset valuation.

In fact, in terms of the brutish persuasiveness of statistics, it can easily be argued that if significance in design can be measured in terms of economic activity, then corporate identity consultants, graphic designers, packaging experts, advertising agents and whoever else is responsible for the *appearance* of KitKat, Rolo and whatever other brand, are at least as important as the product designers of those more innocent yester-years. It was the fiercely contested takeover of Rowntree by Nestlé which brought brand valuation under public scrutiny, making people aware of the strange forces which influence modern business. When in late 1988 the food processing company Rank-Hovis McDougal valued its brands it was able to add nearly £700m to its balance sheet. Some have christened this 'voodoo economics'.

8 In modern takeovers the cost of 'goodwill' (the difference between a fair price, admittedly subjective, and the price paid) is often considerable. When Grand Metropolitan bought Heublein in 1987 it paid nearly £800m for a company whose assets were only £200m. The difference was accounted for by the value of Heublein's portfolio of attractive brands.

Meanwhile, newspapers debated whether this was 'imprecise reality' or 'precise fiction'. Supporters claimed that it was realistic, since putting a price on 'goodwill' reduces grounds for acrimonious exchange in the event of a takeover.[8] Accountants were often hostile, questioning the prudence about investments in imagery and muttering and tutting net and gross, but graphic designers, corporate identity consultants and advertising agents were delighted to have their work so highly valued.

The business of brand valuation involves niceties of accounting and financial ideas that approach metaphysics in their complexity and irrelevance to day-to-day

125. Cotton printing was the first modern reproduction technology, requiring both patterns to be simplified and designs to be protected.

126. The KitKat brand, rather than the chocolate or the factory that makes it, was valued at hundreds of millions when Nestlé took over Rowntree in 1988.

125

126

128

127

129

130

127. Sony's 1988 advertisement wittily reverses the assumption that hardware is nowadays worth more than software.

128, 129. Japanese factories now have process efficiency at such high levels that their flexibility encourages creativity, undermining the traditional role of the industrial designer. Their car industry has rapidly closed the gap between themselves and the Europeans. Toyota MR2 (1985).

130. Raymond Loewy in 1939.

operations, but the meaning is very considerable. The late twentieth century is the stage of one of the most extraordinary dramas in the history of civilisation, a drama whose meaning undermines all historical assumptions about tradition, value and meaning (to say nothing of the role of the designer and his colleagues in media services).

The plot of this drama is very simple, its meaning less so. The plot is this: *ideas and images now have more value than artefacts.* To use the metaphors of computing, so relevant to contemporary conditions, software is more significant than hardware. This change is effecting not only high technology industries, but also the old smoke-stack ones. A former Chairman of Quaker Oats said:

> "If this business were to be split up, I would be glad to take the brands, trademarks and goodwill and you could have all the bricks and mortar − and I would fare better than you."

At the moment, brand valuation is more important in stable industries producing low technology consumer products, especially food-processing, where simple brands − Coke, Mars, Foster's − neatly define simple products. But soon more sophisticated consumer goods, electronics and vehicles, for instance, will reach the level of technological stability now found in soft drinks, chocolate bars and beer. When this happens, the value of the brand, established by a tradition of excellence in product design and enforced by strong graphics, will become valuable in itself.

For instance, in the vehicle industry there is a global trend towards sharing components both among the different territorial divisions of multi-nationals and even among rivals in world markets. Already, some Volvos have Volkswagon engines, Rovers have Honda gearboxes and even some Fords use major components from Peugeot. Eventually, according to an internal Ford policy paper, the position will be "common product development, component commonality, and worldwide sourcing flexibility".[9] Design will help manufacturers satisfy "unique customer requirements for each market destination." But while it may yet be improbable, the possibility exists that one day vehicles will all be the same, differentiated only by *design*. When this happens, techniques of brand valuation will be applied to automobile industry balance sheets and only then will someone be able to put a price on the value of any particular manufacturing tradition.

[9] Leaked to the *Financial Times*, 5th January 1989.

The gentle shift from software to hardware can be seen everywhere. Even in Japan. While Japanese mastery of industrial processes continues to get more expert, some companies are already responding to the new emphasis on software. Their own efficiencies have, indeed, stimulated ever more astonishing creative achievements, but they have also reduced the costs.[10] Conventionally, Japanese manufacturers compensate for reduced costs by adding more and more 'features' to a product, but there are limits to how much 'added value' the customer can take. Indeed, in some product areas there is evidence that his appetite is sated. So, Japanese companies are beginning to invest in software.

[10] See Essay #20.

Among the first was Sony, so properly a leader in the post-industrial age as it was a leader in technology, marketing and the formal aspects of design in the last years of the past age. While a good deal of the argument in favour of Sony's acquisition of CBS in October 1987 was that with a huge video library, it could in a future standards war, force its choice of format onto the global market, the underlying argument is more insidious, going back to that huckster's principle *give away the razor, sell the blades.*

The first generation of consultant industrial designers who set up their studios in New York in the twenties spoke wistfully about 'the cash value of art' as a way of justifying the time spent and the fees charged for streamlining American manufacturing businesses. In sixty years the industrial process has changed so much it would be unrecognisable to Raymond Loewy or Henry Dreyfuss, but increasing automation has not diminished the role of the designer, more simply it has changed it.[11] More than Loewy or Dreyfuss could ever have dreamed, design has become the cash-value-of-art.

Stable industries, whether food, vehicles or manufacturing, need more design... not less.

11   One interesting footnote to the 'cash-value-of-art' thesis was provided by the Policy Studies Institute Report on *The Economic Importance of the Arts in Britain*, 1988; which estimated £4bn invisible earnings from the arts.

131

131. The drafting room at
the Bell Laboratories.

132. Ferranti 'Mark 1'
mainframe computer
(1952). Early computers
filled entire buildings. Now
much of the technology is
contained in a single micro
chip.

132

AS WE MAY THINK
Vannevar Bush

Bush (1895-1974) was a member of the 'Manhattan Project', the team which created the atomic bomb. He is better remembered for his work on computers, beginning in the twenties when he started to develop an analogue computer in the tradition of Charles Babbage. 'As We May Think' was originally published in *Atlantic Monthly*. Its optimistic mood might be a form of expiation for the Manhatten Project which came to prominence in the same year, demonstrating to horrific effect the dark side of technology. In his fascinating essay Bush is inching his way towards a description of RAM (Random Access Memory, the brains of current computers), but his vision of the future is constrained by the quaint imagery of electro-mechanical systems. Nevertheless, his description of expert systems is prophetic.

The summation of human experience is being expanded at a prodigious rate, and the means we use for threading through the consequent maze to the momentarily important item is the same as was used in the days of square-rigged ships.

But there are signs of a change as new and powerful instrumentalities come into use. Photocells capable of seeing things in a physical sense, advanced photography which can record what is seen or even what is not, thermionic tubes capable of controlling potent forces under the guidance of less power than a mosquito uses to vibrate its wings, cathode ray tubes rendering visible an occurrence so brief that by comparison a microsecond is a long time, relay combinations which will carry out involved sequences of movements more reliably than any human operator and thousands of times as fast — there are plenty of mechanical aids with which to effect a transformation in scientific records.

Two centuries ago Leibnitz invented a calculating machine which embodied most of the essential features of recent keyboard devices, but it could not then come into use. The economics of the situation were against it: the labour involved in constructing it, before the days of mass-production, exceeded the labour to be saved by its use, since all it could accomplish could be duplicated by sufficient use of pencil and paper. Moreover, it would have been subject to frequent breakdown, so that it could not have been depended upon; for at that time and long after, complexity and unreliability were synonymous.

Babbage, even with remarkably generous support for his time, could not produce his great arithmetical machine. His idea was sound enough, but construction and maintenance costs were then too heavy. Had a Pharaoh been given detailed and explicit designs for an automobile, and had he understood them completely, it would have taxed the resources of his kingdom to have fashioned the thousands of parts for a single car, and that car would have broken down on the first trip to Giza.

Machines with interchangeable parts can now be constructed with great economy of effort. In spite of much complexity, they perform reliably. Witness the humble typewriter, or the movie camera, or the automobile...Note the automatic telephone exchange, which has hundreds of thousands of such contacts, and yet is reliable. A spider web of metal, sealed in a thin glass container, a wire heated to brilliant glow, in short, the thermionic tube of radio sets, is made by the hundred million, tossed about in packages, plugged into sockets — and it works! Its gossamer parts, the precise location and alignment involved in its construction, would have occupied a master craftsman of the guild for months; now it is built for thirty cents. The world has arrived at an age of cheap complex devices of great reliability; and something is bound to come of it.

The human mind operates by association. With one item in its grasp, it snaps instantly to the next that is suggested by the association of thoughts, in accordance with some intricate web of trails carried by the cells of the brain. It has other characteristics, of course; trails that are not frequently followed are prone to fade, items are not fully permanent, memory is transitory. Yet the speed of action, the intricacy of trails, the detail of mental pictures, is awe-inspiring beyond all else in nature.

Man cannot hope fully to duplicate this mental process artificially, but he certainly ought to be able to learn from it. In minor ways he may even improve, for his records have relative permanency. The first idea, however, to be drawn from the analogy concerns selection. Selection by association, rather than by indexing, may yet be mechanized. One cannot hope thus to equal the speed and flexibility with which the mind follows an associative trail, but it should be possible to beat the mind decisively in regard to the permanence and clarity of the items resurrected from storage.

Consider a future device for individual use, which is a sort of mechanized private file and library. It needs a name, and, to coin one at random 'memex' will do. A memex is a device in which an individual stores all his books, records, and communications, and which is mechanized so that it may be consulted with exceeding speed and flexibility. It is an enlarged intimate supplement to his memory.

It consists of a desk, and while it can presumably be operated from a distance, it is primarily the piece of furniture at which he works. On the top are slanting translucent screens, on which material can be projected for convenient reading. There is a keyboard, and sets of buttons and levers. Otherwise it looks like an ordinary desk.

In one end is the stored material. The matter of bulk is well taken care of by improved microfilm. Only a small part of the interior of the memex is devoted to storage, the rest to mechanism. Yet if the user inserted 5000 pages of material a day it would take him hundreds of years to fill the repository, so he can be profligate and enter material freely.

Most of the memex contents are purchased on micro-film ready for insertion. Books of all sorts, pictures, current periodicals, newspapers, are thus obtained and dropped into place. Business correspondence takes the same path. And there is provision for direct entry. On the top of the memex is a transparent platen. On this are placed longhand notes, photographs, memoranda, all sorts of things. When one is in place, the depression of a lever causes it to be photographed onto the next blank space in a section of the memex film, dry photography being employed.

There is, of course, provision for consultation of the record by the usual scheme of indexing. If the user wishes to consult a certain book, he taps its code on the keyboard, and the title page of the book promptly appears before him, projected onto one of his viewing positions. Frequently used codes are mnemonic, so that he seldom consults his code book; but when he does, a single tap of a key projects it for his use. Moreover, he has supplemental levers. On deflecting one of these levers to the right he runs through the book before him, each page in turn being projected at a speed which just allows a recognising glance at each. If he deflects it further to the right, he steps through the book ten pages at a time; still further at a hundred pages at a time. Deflection to the left gives him the same control backwards.

A special button transfers him immediately to the first page of the index. Any given book of his library can thus be called up and consulted with far greater facility than if it were taken from a shelf. As he has several projection positions, he can leave one item in position while he calls up another. He can add marginal notes and comments, taking advantage of one possible type of dry photography, and it could even be arranged so that he can do this by a stylus scheme, such as is now employed in the telautograph seen in railroad waiting rooms, just as though he had the physical page before him.

All this is conventional, except for the projection forward of present-day mechanisms and gadgetry. It affords an immediate step, however, to associative indexing, the basic idea of which is a provision whereby any item may be caused at will to select immediately and automatically another. This is the essential feature of the memex. The process of tying two items together is the important thing.

When the user is building a trail, he names it, inserts the name in his code book, and taps it out on his keyboard. Before him are the two items to be joined, projected onto adjacent viewing positions. At the bottom of each there are a number of blank code spaces, and a pointer is set to indicate one of these on each item. The user taps a single key, and the items are permanently joined. In each code space appears the code word. Out of view, but also in the code space, is inserted a set of dots for photocell viewing; and on each item these dots by their positions designate the index number of the other item.

Thereafter, at any time, when one of these items is in view, the other can be instantly recalled merely by tapping a button below the corresponding code space. Moreover, when numerous items have been thus joined together to form a trail, they can be reviewed in turn, rapidly or slowly, by deflecting a lever like that used for turning the pages of a book. It is exactly as though the physical items had been gathered together from widely separated sources and bound together to form a new book. It is more than this, for any item can be joined into numerous trails.

The owner of the memex, let us say, is interested in the origin and properties of the bow and arrow. Specifically he is studying why the short Turkish bow was apparently superior to the English long bow in the skirmishes of the Crusades. He has dozens of possibly pertinent books and articles in his memex. First he runs through an encyclopaedia, finds an interesting but sketchy article, leaves it projected. Next, in a history, he finds another pertinent item, and ties the two together. Thus he goes, building a trail of many items. Occasionally he inserts a comment of his own, either linking it into the main trail or joining it by a side trail to a particular item. When it becomes evident that the elastic properties of available materials had a great deal to do with the bow, he branches off on a side trail which takes him through textbooks on elasticity and tables of physical constants. He inserts a page of longhand analysis of his own. Thus he builds a trail of his interest through the maze of materials available to him.

Wholly new forms of encyclopaedias will appear, ready-made with a mesh of associative trails running through them, ready to be dropped into the memex and there amplified. The lawyer has at his touch the associated opinions and decisions of his whole experience, and of the experience of friends and authorities. The patent attorney has on call the millions of issued patents, with familiar trails to every point of his client's interest. The physician, puzzled by a patient's reactions, strikes the trail established in studying an earlier similar case, and runs rapidly through analogous case histories, with side references to the classics for the pertinent anatomy and histology. The chemist, struggling with the synthesis of an organic compound, has all the chemical literature before him in his laboratory, with trails following the analogyes of compounds, and side trails to their physical and chemical behaviour.

The historian, with a vast chronological account of a people, parallels it with a skip trail which stops only on the salient items, and can follow at any time contemporary trails which lead him all over civilization at a particular epoch. There is a new profession of trail blazers, those who find delight in the task of establishing useful trails through the enormous mass of the common record. The inheritance from the master becomes, not only his additions to the world's record, but for his disciples the entire scaffolding by which they were erected.

Thus science may implement the ways in which man produces, stores, and consults the record of the race. It might be striking to outline the instrumentalities of the future more spectacularly, rather than to stick closely to methods and elements now known and undergoing rapid development, as has been here. Technical difficulties of all sorts have been ignored, certainly, but also ignored are means as yet unknown which may come any day to accelerate technical programmes as violently as did the advent of the thermionic tube. In order that the picture may not be too commonplace, by reason of sticking to present-day patterns, it may be well to mention one such possibility, not to prophesy but merely to suggest, for prophecy based on extension of the known as substance, while prophecy founded on the unknown is only a doubly involved guess.

All our steps in creating or absorbing material of the record proceed through one of the senses — the tactile when we touch keys, the oral when we speak or listen, the visual when we read. Is it not possible that some day the path may be established more directly?

THE HABIT OF PLEASURE

John Thackara

Thackara (*b*.1951) is managing director of Design Analysis International, a consultancy based in London and Tokyo. A former editor of *Design* magazine, Thackara is also a visiting tutor at the Royal College of Art. In this essay Thackara develops the idea rehearsed in his lectures and his books, *New British Design* (1986) and *Design After Modernism* (1988), that in future design will become 'knowledge engineering'.

'*W*hat's dark and knocks at the door?' 'The Future'.

The 1980s have made it fashionable to proclaim the 'end of progress' in culture, which is defined increasingly as the sum of the things we consume. This brings to mind the story of Buridan's Ass: the French scholastic told of a donkey which starved to death while trying to decide which of two equally delicious piles of food to eat; Buridan's Ass is surely the archetypal 1980s consumer befuddled by the variety and constant change that makes shopping – for goods, or for ideas – so stressful.

At one level, things do look bad. It has become common to complain that we have too much change, too much consumption; if this is 'progress', the arguments go, then we've had enough of it. Typical of the mood is this Silicon Valley yuppie who complains: "It hardly matters what I buy, I just get a kick out of buying...It's like that first whiff of cocaine, I just get higher and higher as I buy."[1]

[1] *Processed World*, 23.

Marketing guru James Ogilvy, saying little to dispel the yuppie's paranoia, describes consumerism as "anything you can do to your mind with a product or service...people look at products as if they were mind-altering substances."[2]

[2] op. cit.

Technology in general, and design in particular, are among the more prominent targets of a fast-developing backlash against consumerism. Although its members are a motley alliance, ranging from radical ecologists, who would have us halt industrial production at once, to ultra-conservative aestheticians, who would abolish Modern Art even more promptly, this nascent puritanism nonetheless poses a fair question: do we really need *more 'creativity', or have we had enough?*

It is symptomatic of our current disassociation from history that we should imagine this debate to be a novel one. Baudelaire identified a link between fashion and death during the nineteenth century when he observed: "Living matter, you are nothing more than the fixed heart of chaos". And Karl Marx's famous observation that "all that is solid turns into air"[3] concluded his analysis of a perpetual motion consumption system which, although dramatically intensified by industrialisation, has roots which lie in the earliest origins of economic man. What alters through time are the nature and intensity of our consumption – not the fact that we consume.

[3] The quote was later taken as the title of an important book on the meanings of modernism by Marshall Berman *All That is Solid Melts into Air*, 1983.

Critics of modern design and marketing say we have got 'sensuality on the brain', that our economic system produces new and quite artificial 'needs' which can never be satisfied (see W. F. Haug's analysis of commodity aesthetics. Essay #16). Design, so the argument goes, invests quite ordinary products with a glamour and mystique that only heightens the disappointment we experience when finally we possess them. Thus in

America, where adults average six hours of shopping each week (as against forty minutes playing with their children), forty per cent of shoppers say they have 'quite a lot' of unopened purchases stored at home. But strictly speaking it is not design, or even materialism, that drives such behaviour; as Processed World *puts it: "from the technical sophistication of a 'dress watch', to the durability of ballistics-grade travel luggage, to the purity of the organically grown tomato, people are shopping for qualities that make them feel secure in an unstable world."*

In this psycho-social context, technology is the occasion *for continuous innovation, (and the pathology of overconsumption); and design is its* means; *neither, however, is its* cause.

The role of technology in our daily traffic with things is more complex than the conspiracy theory of consumption which imagines design interacting with technology to create superfluous novelty for its own sake. This theory is based on the spurious premise of a 'rational economic man' who would restrict himself to a bare minimum of food and equipment if he were not seduced by the dark forces of commerce. As social anthropologists are now beginning to discover, this view ignores both the social and psychological dimension of consumption. Peter Lloyd Jones explains that modern man has "the habit of pleasure...only by understanding the social, as well as the technical dimension of consumption can we understand that the 'functions' people want in their daily lives are not just technical, but psychological ones too".[4] Lloyd Jones goes on to describe the ways in which the 'seduction of pleasure', and our 'addiction to comfort', are as much a part of the aesthetic impulse as are hunger, or the need for warmth.

4 *Things and People*
(unpublished manuscript;
Kingston Polytechnic,
London).

Although some specialists say it is possible actually to measure the so-called aesthetic impulse in consumption – and the literature abounds with such enticing terms as 'hedonic indexes' and the 'Wundt satisfaction curves' – a yawning gap continues to isolate design practice from the behavioural sciences. Design seems intimidated by the 'messiness' of the territory on which the scientific or technological world, with which it is confident, and the study of behaviour, with which it is not, overlaps. One cannot measure behaviour as one might measure a radius, or for that matter a pixel; behaviour resists attempts to impose rational order and quantitative techniques.

It is in its failure creatively to bridge the worlds of science, behaviour and aesthetics that the crisis of modern design lies – not in consumerism per se. For its part, science is changing, even dramatically, in the direction of inter-disciplinary research; but design, stranded in a backwater, along with many of the fine arts, is in what Anthony Hill calls an "entropic state...(displaying) neither intensive research nor any movement towards unification. Meanwhile the athletic mind turns to the past, constantly reshuffling a pack which cannot be claimed to be complete."[5]

5 *Art Monthly*, February
1989.

The failure to translate the raw material of science and technology into desirable products has been described as the 'innovation gap' – a phenomenon whose dire consequences for the economics of Europe and America provoke constant cries of anguish among technologists and government mandarins. But despite endless talk of the need to change attitudes, little concrete action has ensued: even the most sophisticated cultural engineers now concede that 'economic behaviour is more enigmatic even than sexuality.'[6]

6 Meaghan Morris 'Banality
in Cultural Studies', *Block*
Autumn, 1988.

In Japan, where the 'innovation gap' is tiny by comparison with the West – measured in weeks rather than in generations – they take a more rounded, cultural view of the innovation process. Where Western managers bang on about 'leadership' and 'pushing new ideas through', their Japanese counterparts talk about creating fertile 'environments'

135. The challenge facing design in the information age has its precedents: steam engines expressed an engineering aesthetic that transcended simple mechanism; and the design of electrical products entailed 'a complete transformation of our aesthetic notions'.

136. The tertiary technologies turn the modernist adage upside down: now, 'function creates formlessness'. A new design aesthetics must tackle the complexity, abstraction and non-linearity of information systems.

135

136

137

137, 138.The value of software as a proportion of the information economy continues to soar – some hardware is already given away free. But the role of *objects*, as interfaces, as controls, or as totems, will remain crucial. Shown here: an high-tech audio desk designed by Nick Oakley.

138

109

wherein new products may be 'born' as the progeny of a culture in which tradition and innovation co-exist in harmony. Sharp's enlightened design chief, Kyoshi Sakashita, compares the two attitudes to 'the sword and the vase...the one being aggressive, the other receptive.'[7]

7 Address to the Regional Design Conference; Fukuyama, Japan; November 1988.

Although there is much talk of a new era in technology, a 'tertiarisation'[8] of products become intangible, and incorporeal information systems are distributed around the world, the basic contradiction between what is technically possible, and what is comprehensible or desirable to consumers, has been a recurrent feature of the industrial landscape. Back in 1903, for example, AEG's Paul Westheim observed at the dawn of electricity that "in order to make a lucid, logical and clearly articulated entity out of an arc lamp, a complete transformation of our aesthetic notions was necessary."[9] Throughout the history of modern science, in other words, the creative aspect of the design process has involved a degree of cultural and psychological sensitivity that is given insufficient prominence in the textbooks and curriculums.

8 'Design and the Age of Quality', *Design*, April 1983.

9 Tilman Buddenseig and Henning Rogge, *Industriekultur: Peter Behrens and the AEG*, 1984.

That said, some features of today's scientific and technical landscape do pose qualitatively new challenges for design that will not be met by scavenging around in the archives, where tradition has nothing to offer innovation. According to the French critic Thierry Chaput, the very functions of the tertiary information technologies creates formlessness, neatly derailing the original modernist prescription for design that 'form follows function'.[10] We need, says Chaput, a new aesthetic, an aesthetic that can comprehend the complexity, abstraction, and non-linearity that distinguish today's technologies from those that preceded them.

10 *Nouvelles Tendances* (exh. cat., Centre Pompidou, Paris, 1984).

By complexity, Chaput means the replacement of mechanical and electrical 'models' of the machines which fill our lives — models with deep roots in our culture — with new technologies, which, because they are continuously interactive, and 'design themselves' to a degree, cannot be approached with the same conceptual equipment that would be appropriate for a motor, or even a refinery.[11] Abstraction, in turn, is one consequence when information systems are disarticulated in space — by being located in networks whose nodes may be thousands of miles apart. Thirdly, technology becomes non-linear when it is fragmented in time; the notion of 'layered' software programmes, which are sometimes dormant, sometimes alive, undermines the traditional models of causality that informed previous design regimes.

11 John Chris Jones, *Technology Changes*, 1986.

Electricity, too, was 'abstract', in the sense that you could not see or touch it; but it was nonetheless possible for design to derive static symbols for what it did ('light', 'fire', 'motor') from its functions. With software, a new form of dynamic imagery is needed; as someone once said of art, design must 'represent the unpresentable'.

But just because design in the information era is about perception does not mean it will cease to be about things; on the contrary, there is every sign that as the value of software in the modern economy soars, the role of objects — as interfaces, as controls, or as totems — is receiving greater attention. Although the value of software is likely to exceed the value of hardware by seven times in the 1990s,[12] no amount of on-screen gee-wizzardry will replace the physical thing as a powerful icon through and in which we will access these global systems.

12 *Financial Times*, February 1988.

The French Minitel is an excellent example. French policy for telecommunications recognised that the best way to catapult its populace dramatically into the telecommunications mainstream was by giving them the hardware (in this case, an astounding seven million 'intelligent terminals') needed to connect them with the networks. British policy, based on the incremental penetration of information into the home through the commercial (and highly cumbersome) television-based Prestel system, has been a great anti-climax by comparison. France is now the world's leader in the establishment of a third-generation technical-information infrastructure. In neither case, however, have designers been able to impart much magic to what are not, given their potential functions, prosaic objects.

The continuing importance of designed objects is further illustrated by the case of CDRom technology. It is now possible to record vast amounts of data on a single silver disk – 1,000 books, 10,000 books, 100,000 books, it's only a matter of time – and to access this vast database through a single A4-sized, laptop 'reader'. To date, this mind-boggling device has been 'packaged' in the most banal format imaginable – a black box with a screen in it, or about as exciting as a central heating controller (and very similar-looking too). To the boffins, well aware of what lies 'inside', such banality is no deterrent; but to engage the interest of the rest of the likely user-population, reared for years on traditional notions of 'book', something more imaginative will be needed to disseminate the gadget. Unfortunately, such is the impoverishment, overall, of the product design community, that an inspired answer to this, and similar challenges, is not an immediate prospect.

Although most objects emerging from the narrow confines of the design business remain banal, technology, and in particular new materials and processes, is now generating many new opportunities. An important book called The Material of Invention *(1986) by Ezio Manzini, describes the way that technology has given a 'second childhood' to traditional materials; and created opportunities, with non-traditional new composites and processes, such as 'pultrusion', for designers to tackle qualitatively new problems.*

Manzini is explicit: he rejects the tendency of the post modernist 1980s to denigrate the object, and to celebrate abstraction. It is a laughable conceit, says Manzini, for modern man to imagine he has 'grown out of' artefacts when he has barely begun to explore the range of possible objects, technical or otherwise, we might create. "For his first million years, man subsisted on just five materials", Manzini explains; "today, a comprehensive technical dictionary contains 4.5 million entries. Who can possibly argue that we have exhausted the potential of such a resource?"

The properties described in Manzini's analysis of 'transformed' traditional materials, or of invented new ones, correspond in many respects to the abstract qualities of the new technologies described earlier: lightness, transparency, pliability, transformability, elastically. In representing the abstract qualities of the new technology, the physical resources are there for the taking: will designers respond?

If the prevailing culture in which they work persists, the answer is probably no. I recently attended an internal design briefing for the managers of a major computer company at which great play was made of the need to redesign the company's structures, to make them more open, flexible, opaque and generally 'leaky' – the idea being to sensitize their vast bureaucracy to the subtleties of a constantly-changing market-place. I suggested, during this discussion, that the company might look, first, at its corporate architecture policy which favoured two styles: the monolithic, reflecting-mirror type of tower block, on the one hand; and the hidden, camouflaged, and generally mysterious armed camp style that informed its non public facilities. "Oh, we couldn't change that", several managers said; "our image is based on being the biggest and the most powerful company in the marketplace; that is reflected in our buildings".

Substantive progress in the creative relationship between design and technology is heavily dependent on an organisational culture open to new ideas, and supportive of experimentation.[13] *Which, in a competitive market, is easier aspired to than achieved –*

13 **James Fairhead, *Design and Corporate Culture*, 1988.**

111

the day-to-day pressure on managers to achieve results is hard to reconcile with an open environment in which expertise is easily transferred, training continuous and team-work the norm. Hence the recent importance given to the idea of culture or innovation audits, in which senior managers, with or without the help of outside consultants, 'interrogate' their organisation to discover whether the conditions that all agree should, ideally, be met, actually are.

Scientists and engineers, too, persist in patterns of thought and behaviour inimitable to innovation – such as the radical separation of reason from intuition and tacit, everyday experience. In the artificial intelligence community, for example, cyberneticians have taken to arguing that 'creativity' rarely represents any large deviation from 'standard patterns'; the cybernetician James Albus says of creativity, "we take a familiar behavioural trajectory, add a tiny variation, and claim we have discovered something new...(I wonder if) true creativity ever happens at all...it may be argued that all creative arts and insights merely represent rearrangements of elements in experience".

"Rearrangements of elements in experience"...it is by such language that the so-called knowledge engineers demonstrate that for all their expertise, they remain incapable of reflective thought. No doubt many human skills can be codified and digitised and taught to machines, but knowledge engineers, brainwashed by their institutional culture of science or big business, are blind to the real understanding that human beings are, by virtue of their having bodies, interacting skilfully with the material world, and being trained into a culture.

THE FUTURE

Commerce and Culture has looked at a wide range of artistic, social, technical and cultural ideas which have formed the climate of thought in which designers work. But what of the future? Now that the post-modern deregulation of history has demolished the old conviction that at any time there is a single, unifying style which expresses the spirit of the age, now that 'designer' is as pejorative a term as 'executive' or 'de luxe', now that all available aesthetic choice is to be found on somebody or other's computerised expert system, what is there for designers?

Are the designers of the past, one might say, the 'traditional' designers, models for the future? There used to be magazine features showing sleek, pomaded moustachioed creatures like Raymond Loewy. Circa 1962, Loewy posed for pictures, dressed in a white suit, extravagant foulard and spats, posing by the new Studebaker Avanti whose striking body he had just designed. Or Charles Eames, handsome, square-jawed, tough, but sensitive, drop-dead cool. He was in a wash'n'wear plaid shirt, sitting in the artistically cluttered studio of his Venice, California, house. This habitation he made from industrial components. Then take Eliot Noyes, the very picture of New England refinement with his crew cut, his button downs and his Beechcraft. Noyes was the Harvard architect who redesigned the entire appearance of IBM, telling the Chairman in a memorably pithy memorandum announcing his proposals "You would prefer neatness". In the American magazines, Noyes was frequently photographed with his wife, Molly, near their beautiful Connecticut house. They always used to have matching cars: this year Thunderbirds, then Porsche 356s, even Land-Rovers.

And all of this was marvellous, giving a clear impression that design was all about shaping appearance, about changing the look of things. And so in a way it still is, but it has become other things as well and because of that the look of things has moved somewhere else in the system of values where we judge the quality and character of things.

When people talk about design they are talking — more or less consciously — about two things. The first is the simplest to grasp. Design is what a certain group of professionals and artisans do when they engage in making creative decisions about the function and appearance of the things we buy and use. The second is more abstract, but places design on a par, as we have said, with, literature and the fine arts in its status as an activity which defines man's relationship with the material world.

This is design as something which embraces both production and consumption, as it were, the critical intelligence co-ordinating supply and demand. This activity involves both professional designers, manufacturers and — perhaps most importantly — consumers. Few histories involving design have been written, which is not to say that histories of what designers have done are lacking. *Commerce and Culture* is an attempt to lay the basis for such a book so that in future a history of civilisation might be written which is as much concerned with objects as it is with wars.

Commerce and Culture has looked at the relationship of art with the everyday in order to understand what influences consumer choice in a world of rapidly changing technical and social values. This is why it began by examining a work of art created as an artefact and went on to question what real merit lies in traditions when modern technology undermines their cultural basis. Similarly, what deeper structure is suggested by our entrenched attitudes to reproductions? Now that packaging and surface dominate both commerce and culture, is civilization reduced to superficiality?

Museums and department stores are among the most fascinating institutional creations of the last century and a half. By putting the merchandise of the world, past and present, on display they fomented a crisis which has led to the banalisation of art. This crisis culminated in a merger of the two. One other manifestation of the same crisis was the designer cult, with false gods spotlit on plinths. Again, this phenomenon is from the infantile stage of the history of industrial design. To enhance the paradox that the celebration of designer-this and designer-that discredited the notion of design as a serious subject, it need only be mentioned that it was during the designer decade that technology (in the form of expert systems) and process (in the form of fast-track construction) finally undermined traditional attitudes to architecture, mother of the arts and the greatest of the design skills.

Nowadays, design is not simply about appearance, but is increasingly concerned with...*experience*. The most important experience of the twentieth century is speed. Indeed, as Aldous Huxley once remarked, speed is the only entirely novel sensation of our age. Flight, after all, was known in the eighteenth century, if only to the Montgolfier brothers. Speed compresses time and space and is thus both a description of what new technology demands as well as being a metaphor of what new technology does.

Imagine a conversation among leaders of the automobile industry. Eavesdropping ten years ago would have been all about design: the industry men would have been muttering knowingly about its importance, its contribution to the bottom line, to perceived value and all of that. Nowadays they *know* it's important and confer on it that greatest of compliments, of taking it for granted; they would be no more likely to have a heated exchange-of-views about design than they would about any other accepted fact of industrialised capitalist production, such as discounted cash flow or inventory control.

Instead, the know-all mutterings today are about *distribution*. Now that functional and aesthetic excellence are the baseline for any company that expects to survive beyond the end of the week, the real competitive advantage comes from mastery of time and space. You speak to FIAT or Ford or Toyota or Toshiba or Benetton and you will find this is what concerns them most.

In its Castrette warehouse Benetton owns the most sophisticated distribution centre in the world, serving the globe from one building. Benetton does not manufacture a single garment until it is ordered and just as soon as the order is processed your woolly is documented and tracked through the entire manufacturing process all the way into the 280,000 cubic metre warehouse where Comau robots store it and its sibling woollies in a random access system not dissimilar in its complexity and efficiency to a computer's memory.

To the human visitor the system looks bewildering, with boxes for Chelmsford hugger-mugger with boxes for Tokyo, but the computer knows where everything is, sees it onto conveyors, into trucks and speedily to market. Benetton says the whole process takes no more than seventeen days, of which a rigid seven are accounted for by distribution *irrespective of destination*. This system keeps Benetton in constant, direct contact with its stores and turns on their head all the old assumptions about design-for-industry because now the possibility exists, within the amazingly short seventeen day cycle, for designer and manufacturer to be directly responsible to changing public taste. Soon they might start responding, rather than imposing.

139

Benetton has five thousand
shops around the world . . .

140

. . . which it serves from a
single warehouse in
northern Italy.

141

Nothing is manufactured
until it is ordered.

142

The vast warehouse is
organised like a random
access memory. . .

143

. . . with consignments
arranged apparently
haphazardly . . .

144

. . . but a computer controls
the entire distribution
process.

145

Benetton is committed to
refining *distribution*, a
process which now takes it
only seventeen days . . .

146

The potential is that with
such a speedy operation,
the manufacturer can be in
closer touch with the
retailer . . .

147

. . . and the designer in
closer touch with the
consumer.

1   A curious article, 'Long Distance Shopping by Telephone' in the *Daily Mail*, 28th August 1906; explained ''Many villages...are now equipped with a service, thus enabling women to order their household necessities at the great London stores and secure a country life with city conveniences.''

2   John Diebold, by his own account, coined the word 'automation' when he actually failed to spell 'automatization' correctly.

3   See Essay #23

4   Fibrox is an elision of 'fibre-optical', multi-cored, cable carrying digitalised laser information. The present capacity of fibrox is about one thousand times greater than copper wire.

5   Nicholas Negroponte, of the Massachusetts' Institute of Technology's Media Laboratory, says the typical home computer of the future will have the capacity of current Cray supercomputers, capable, for instance, of processing fifty million instructions-per-second, *Forbes*, 20th February 1989.

6   The pharmaceutical company, Smith Kline Beckman, already uses fibrox for 'narrowcasting' of training films to doctors, pharmacist and salesmen.

Since museums and department stores first put the man-made world on display, the public has demanded of all new technologies that they provide a similar service. First it was catalogue showrooms on the Wedgwood model, then it was department stores, then it was the telephone which changed experience.[1] In *Automation* (1952) John Diebold explained that all new technologies, from print through to artificial intelligence, tend to impose the following pattern of changes: (1) Allow you to mechanise what you did yesterday (2) But then you find technology changes the actual task (3) And then changes in society follow.[2]

The latest innovation is teleshopping, a phenomenon that brings the discussion of commerce and culture full circle.[3] Teleshopping has the potential to realise in full the cultural opportunities suggested in André Malraux's idea of a future 'Museum without Walls', while satisfying the commercial appetites of Aristide Boucicaut's 'Bon Marché'. Presently restricted to test markets in the United States, teleshopping could bring the museum and the store into your own home.

Teleshopping depends not only on the consumer's appetite, but also on two new technologies: *fibrox*,[4] and the fast-approaching integration of computers and video. Presently, telecommunication companies are laying fibrox cable for voice and data transmission but they are anxious to acquire 'entertainment' too, since the capacity of fibrox allows the carriage of video as well as voice and numbers.

At the same time television receivers are slowly becoming integrated with computers. Presently they have something in common, both televisions and most computer screens are using old-fashioned cathode ray tubes, but by the early 1990s the new machines will use new technology to combine high-definition image processing with vast computing power.[5] The tv-computers will work through fibrox, carrying not only 'traditional' television, but also educational and commercial material.[6]

But other applications of speed will have a crucial influence on design. For about three decades after 1945 the Japanese devoted most of their considerable ingenuity and organisational energy to process efficiency rather than innovation. This characteristically long-term view has now endowed them with an investment of factories so bewilderingly efficient that creativity actually comes out of the shop-floor. It is like a calculus: the Japanese have some brilliant designs not simply because they have brilliant designers, but because they can manufacture anything imaginable.

In Europe even the most advanced manufacturing companies, Volkswagon for instance, have product life cycles of about eight years. The Japanese motor industry is approaching twenty-four months and electronic products are, in some cases, down to a matter of weeks. When you learn that Hitachi manufactures video recorders in ninety seconds, you realise that the Japanese are driving themselves up a helix of efficiency which actually forces creativity. You also realise that the example of Raymond Loewy, Charles Eames and Eliot Noyes are as remote from contemporary issues as Grinling Gibbons or Hepplewhite.

Some Western manufacturers are catching up: Motorola now makes its pagers in two hours when before it used to take three weeks. Hewlett-Packard too has learnt the lesson of the Japanese. Chief Executive, John Young, says:

"Doing it fast forces you to do it right first time".

Thus industrial designers are exposed to Darwinian disciplines hitherto more familiar to racing drivers. With this new emphasis on distribution, time, space and the innovation cycle, aesthetics seem as quaint as 'ars longa vita brevis' did to General Motors in the fifties...or is this going too far, too fast? The old focussed transfer lines

148

149

148 – 150. Mario Bellini
and his influential Olivetti
ET111 (1982). Bellini
believes that the established
role of the industrial
designer (on the model of
Eliot Noyes and IBM,
bottom left) is redundant.
Since technology is not so
overwhelming, designers
will concentrate on 'the art
of living in a home'.

151. In that home there will
be teleshopping, shrinking
time and space into a VDU.
Teleshopping was predicted
by the *Daily Mail* in 1906,
a fascinating early response
to the telephone.

152. Fibrox cable will allow
telephone companies to
transmit huge volumes of
voice, data, and
entertainment, bringing
commerce *and* culture into
the home.

151

150

152

and the principles of linear production established by Henry Ford produced a very particular aesthetic; designers reacted to the disciplines of mass production by developing a visual language whose vocabulary included things like cut-lines, proportions, radii, mouldings. But the new industrial divinity is not manufacturing, but speed. Eventually, when the awareness of this reshuffle seeps into culture, the divinity will have idols made in its image. God used to be in the details, but now he's in the fast lane. When he pulls in for a breather, the Loewy, Eames and Noyes of the next generation are going to be waiting for him.

Certainly, industrial design is going to change. Mario Bellini is one of Italy's greatest product designers, the man responsible for many shapes that have so rapidly gained acceptance that they have become a modern vernacular. Astonishingly, he has said that the term 'industrial design' is redundant,[7] believing that it is futile to separate it from any other type of design activity, whether that is architecture, laying the table or hairdressing. Having been one of the first to realise that miniaturised electronics liberated product designers from slavish adherence to form-following-function, Bellini was also aware that while consumer durables offer ever more attractive superficial features, in real terms they offer less and less. It is, as Wilheim Alff observed, only a matter of time before product design breaks entirely from 'reality'.[8]

The potency of technology allows designers to be purely creative, using both the vast repository of material generated by thousands of years of civilisation, but also potentially making new discoveries on the way. Bellini says that the product itself is now more important than the process.

> "I think it is very positive this new crossing between pure art and applied art and design, because this interchange will nourish both the user's culture and the designer's culture."

As an architect himself, Bellini is well aware that the most satisfactory twentieth-century furniture was designed by architects. As a consultant to Olivetti he is equally aware of the momentous changes technology will impose on the organisation of work...but not necessarily on life. On the contrary, the future seems to hold more and better opportunities for designers and Bellini is only speaking for the Spirit of the Age, or at least for his entire generation, when he says what he most keenly anticipates is a general return to the 'culture of living in a house'.

In this interpretation, design will become more closely involved with the aesthetic and spiritual needs of consumers, perhaps less with the immediate short term goals of manufacturers. Technology will be liberating: there will be data entry by handwriting and IBM even suggests that the electronic 'book' of the future could be leather-bound. The man who invented the silicon chip[9] says that by 2000 the everyday DRAM (Dynamic Random Access Memory) will be more than two hundred times more powerful than the chips which drive today's fastest computers. These, working with optical liquid crystals memories, storing data in three dimensions, will make design research possible in areas people don't yet realise exist.

More than seventy years ago the great Swedish authority on design, Gregor Paulssen,[10] the man who virtually created single-handed the Scandinavian design ethic, said that the essentials of a civilised society are cultivated manufacturers working with intelligent artists to make better products. The end of the old adversary relations of commerce and culture has not yet realised this happy state, but promises it. New technology will make it possible.

7 In *Design* no. 481, 1989.

8 In *Der Begriff des Faschismus*, 1971.

9 Robert N. Noyce of Intel.

10 Director of the Svenska Sljodforeningen and author of the influential *Vackrare Vardagsvara* ('More Beautiful Everyday Things'), 1919.

TELESHOPPING

James Woudhuysen

Woudhuysen (*b.*1952) is Director of Research for Fitch-RS, a London consultancy specialising in retail design.

In Clearwater, Florida, the live TV show compare glances at a computer monitor off-stage. His eulogy for the sparkling rings and bracelets he has in close-up is, the monitor reveals, bringing in sales of $700 a minute. In front of him 1,200 telephone operators in soundproof cubicles take the calls from up to three million homes. Multiply that $700-a-minute figure by all the minutes in a day, and America's Home Shopping Network will rack up sales of hundreds of millions of dollars a year − on this, one of the three TV channels it runs coast-to-coast.

In White Plains, upstate New York, the top executives at Prodigy a 700-strong subsidiary of IBM and Sears Roebuck, are optimistic. They launched a floppy disk and telephone gadget ('modem') which allows users of IBM or IBM-compatible machines not just to shop for airline tickets and Polaroid cameras, but also to follow their favourite news, their local weather and − inevitably − the fortunes of their shares. The Prodigy package sells at $150 for half a year's usage; thereafter, the whole service costs but $9.95 a month to rent. Glistening ads, which fill much of the bottom part of every page you view, underwrite the prices.

These two examples cover the full gamut of buying from the privacy of your own home. Home Shopping Network is based on broadcast, cable and satellite television channels, price-slashing discounts and purchases made on impulse. You never know what will be up for sale next, and you can only get it while it's on the screen. HSN also provide viewers more with showbiz than genuine interactivity: you can phone in, live, to tell a nationwide audience how you just love that tiara, but, apart from using your touchpad telephone to confirm that you'll pay for it to arrive on your doorstep within four days (press 1 to go ahead, 2 for not to), the sense of being connected ends there.

By contrast with HSN, Prodigy caters for considered usage, and wires your PC up to impressive effect too. You can tab across a relatively primitive diagram of that Polaroid camera to have its various features highlighted and explained before you ask for a brochure − or the item itself − to be delivered. You can peruse every ad in more depth, though each decision to do so will be logged on a distant mainframe computer. Most important, you can key in questions about your waistline to Jane Fonda, or at least to her staff. They'll get back to you within seventy-two hours.

Every teleshopping system is different. Take France. There, one of the early acts of President Mitterrand's regime was to distribute to the populace terminals and keyboards designed as a free, electronic substitute for telephone directories. More than three million Minitels now figure in homes and businesses as far-flung as France's overseas territories in the Indian Ocean.

In the late 1970s and early 1980s, a series of teleshopping initiatives in Britain went wrong. Entrepreneurs of the 'wouldn't it be great if?' school introduced expensive, primitive equipment to small, unsuspecting audiences and saw their investments vanish within a year or two. They offered groceries which were neither fresh nor profitable as well as goods and services far too limited in terms of consumer choice. As a result, the

154

154, 155. In America home
shopping is available twenty
four hours a day to more
than twenty six million
householders (top and
bottom).

155

hype that often surrounded teleshopping was exposed as just that; even today, many commentators remain sceptical.

So much money has shifted out of manufacturing and into retailing that conventional retailers, emboldened by a seemingly unstoppable consumer boom, now face a situation in which markets may soon be saturated and trading space is almost impossible to come by. Second, increasing competition between retailers and manufacturers has made the latter anxious to redress the balance of commercial power in their favour; if they can find a way to cut out the middlemen, they will take it. Third, the deregulation of broadcasting and telecommunications opens up opportunities for reaching consumers in new ways. Finally, the individualism, social atomisation and spread in home ownership of the 1980s have, together with the ageing of the population, encouraged a pervasive 'homecentredness' on the part of the British.

Whatever the impact on Britain's worsening trade figures, the possibility of British consumers ordering liver sausage, parmesan and the odd crate of Heineken direct from continental producers — through fibre-optic cable, satellite TV or international telephone lines — is a genuine one. Already, France's Minitel is hooked up to the United States; and, in non-interactive ventures, American and Italian exporters have arranged vast off-the-screen and off-the-page selling sprees to homes in Japan and other overseas locations.

In teleshopping, it appears, anything may be possible. Already tons of personalised junk mail land on British doormats: backed by Orwellian credit card databases recording where and when we last bought what, this 'direct marketing' is but one portent of the commercial power that teleshopping concerns — multinationals, perhaps — may one day wield. Another is what has happened to mail order catalogues, in the era of Bymail *and* Next Directory. *These glossy numbers suggest that teleshopping will not be a habit confined to computer buffs. Last, there are applications more redolent of social responsibility. France's Minitel, for example, now features a medical Expert System which will interrogate you on every symptom once you've keyed in the magic phrase 'I HAVE A HEADACHE'.*

So who will benefit from teleshopping, and in what way? Despite the hedonistic associations of much of the new mail order, to imagine that only the affluent or the youthful will be prepared to learn the discipline would be to prejudge the issue.

But it is not just yuppies who have trouble packing a trip to the shops into a normal week. For both sexes, a lowly sector like manufacturing has seen working hours lengthen since the early 1980s, while the general trend toward part-time work among mothers suggests a similarly intensive, minute-to-minute battle to organise their lives around care for children and the elderly. In a Britain of worsening traffic congestion and — in many places — continuing tensions on the inner city high street, the 'convenience' aspects of selecting by screen are not to be trifled with.

For those lucky enough to retire in some comfort to the country, on the other hand, there may be time enough to engage in a more leisurely type of teleshopping, or the bargain-hunter's comparison of one luxury piece of fashion against another. Here, rural remoteness may make older people some of the biggest teleshopping spenders.

There will be other benefits, too. You might arrange to be reminded of anniversaries; of shampoo bottles running dry; you could, perhaps, engage in electronics haggling, digital barter and much else besides. Certainly, access to the very latest products and services would be made much faster.

121

But for all this to happen, the demanding British consumers, weaned on the punchy presentation of News at Ten and the charts of Newsnight, will have to have their high visual expectations satisfied. Clothes must arrive in the right size, in the colour and condition and at the time you expect them to; but unless they are sold as entertainingly as they are at Britain's gleaming new department stores, you may never feel the urge to order them up.

In teleshopping, as in the tobacconist's on the corner, the customer is always right. When Britain's designers, advertising agencies, television producers and film directors turn their attentions to the new challenges it throws up, overseas teleshopping interests are bound to take note. Then this country may have a new earner of invisible exports, and one much more lucrative than Jewel in the Crown *and* Chariots of Fire.

A F T E R W O R D

Japanese tourists queue to be photographed at the fish counter in Harrods Food Halls, as they still do in front of Buckingham Palace. Museums are considering ways to licence their collections and turn them into consumable merchandise. Some bleary-eyed observers wonder if nowadays anything is real. They long for the moral and aesthetic certainties and convictions of Ruskin, Cole and Morris. With everything available to the consumer, is everything quantifiable only in terms of the yen, the mark or the dollar?

But maybe there are some hardening absolutes in the frothy miasma of availability which the elision of commerce and culture has brought about. If such things exist, they will only ever be identified by a better educated and a more discriminating consumer, provided with information, images and ideas that were hitherto inaccessible or unrelated. It is for him and her that the Design Museum was created.

156. Museums and stores are products of the same nineteenth-century urban civilisations. At the end of the twentieth century the distinction between them has blurred, as Louis Helliman's *Architects' Journal* cartoon wittily suggests.

156

BIBLIOGRAPHY

Atkinson, F., 'La Rinascente Store Rome', *Architectural Review*, no. 788, 1962.

Baker, Malcolm, *The Cast Courts* (Victoria and Albert Museum, London, 1982).

Banham, R., 'HM Fashion House', *The New Statesman*, 27th January 1961.

Bayley, Stephen, 'Can Art Run at a Profit?', *Campaign*, 1st July 1988.

Berger, John, *Ways of Seeing* (London, 1972).

Berman, Marshall, *All that is Solid Melts into Air: Experience of Modernity* (London, 1983).

Boime, Albert, *The Academy and French Paintings in the Nineteenth Century* (London, 1971).

Boorstein, Daniel, *The Decline of Radicalism: Reflections on America Today* (Chicago, 1963).

Brookner, Anita, *Watteau* (London, 1967).

Bonython, Elizabeth, *King Cole: A Picture Portrait of Sir Henry Cole KCB, 1808-1882* (London, 1982).

Chippendale, Thomas, *Gentleman and Cabinet-Makers Directory* (1754).

Cieply, Michael, 'Sony's Profitless Prosperity', *Forbes*, 24th October 1983.

Clark, Hazel, 'The Design and Designing of Lancashire Printed Calicoes During the First Half of the Nineteenth Century', *Textile History*, 15, 1984.

Clausen, Meredith L., *Frantz Jourdain and the Samaritaine: Art Nouveau Theory and Criticism* (Washington, 1987).

Dana, John Cotton, *The New Relations of Museums and Industry* (Newark Museum Asssociation, New Jersey, 1910).

d'Avenel, George, 'Democratisation of Luxury', *Le Mécanisme de la Vie Moderne* (Paris, 1898).

Dickens, Charles, 'A House Full of Horrors', *Household Words*, vol. VI, 1852.

Dutton, E. P. and Tomkins, Calvin, *Merchants and Masterpieces: The Story of the Metropolitan Museum of Art* (New York, 1970).

The Economic Importance of the Arts in Britain (Policy Studies Institute, 1988).

Fairhead, James, *Design and Corporate Culture* (London, 1988).

Ferry, J. W., *A History of the Department Store* (New York, 1960).

Ferry, Jeffrey, 'A Tale of Two Telecoms: The French Connection Keeps Brits Hanging on', *Arena*, July/August 1988.

Gombrich, E. H., *In Search of Cultural History* (Oxford, 1978).

Goncourt, E. and J., *French XVIII Century Painters* (London, 1948).

Guadet, Julian, *Elements et Théories de l'Architecture* (Paris, 1902).

Gubernick, Lisa, 'Marketing: The Good Housekeeping Seal for Hip', *Forbes*, 28th April 1989.

Hald, Arthur and Skawonius, Sven, *Contemporary Swedish Design* (Stockholm, 1951).

Halpern, Kenneth, *Downtown USA: Urban Design in Nine American Cities* (London, 1978).

Haskell, F. and Penny, N., *Taste and the Antique* (London, 1981).

Huxtable, Ada Louise, 'Deep in the Heart of Nowhere', *New York Times*, 15th February 1976.

Jones, Owen, *The Grammar of Ornament* (London, 1856).

Laidlow, Christine, 'The Metropolitan Museum of Art and Modern Design, 1917-1929', *Journal of Decorative and Propaganda Arts*, Spring 1988.

Lyotard, Jean-François, *The Postmodern Condition: A Report on Knowledge* (Manchester, 1984).

Macdonald, Sally, 'For Swines of Discretion: Design for Living', *Museums Journal*, no. 3, December 1986 [Describes Thomas Horsfall's experiment].

Mayor, A. Hyatt, 'Mail Orders in the Eighteenth Century', *Antiques*, October 1975.

Minihan, Janet, *The Nationalization of Culture* (London, 1977).

Miller, M. B., *The Bon Marché: Bourgeois Culture and the Department Store, 1869-1920* (New Jersey, 1981).

Morris, Meaghan, 'Banality in Cultural Studies', *Block*, Autumn 1988.

Marrey, Bernard, *Les Grands Magasins* (Paris, 1979).

Muthesius, Stefan, 'Why Do We Buy Old Furniture? Aspects of the Authentic Antique in Britain, 1870-1910', *Art History*, no. 2, June 1988.

Panofsky, Erwin, *Renaissance and Renascences in Western Art* (London, 1960).

Pevsner, Nikolaus, *A History of Building Types* (London, 1984).

Physick, John, *The Victoria and Albert Museum: The History of its Building* (London, 1982).

Price, Jonathan, *The Best Things on TV* (New York, 1979).

Read, Herbert, *Art and Industry* (London, 1934).

Russell, Gordon, 'What is Good Design?', *Design*, no. 1, January 1949.

Russell, Gordon, *A Designer's Trade* (London, 1968).

Seznac, Jean, *La Survivance des Dieux Antiques* (Paris, 1940).

Sloan Allen, James, *The Romance of Commerce and Culture* (Chicago, 1983).

Stamp, G., Summerson, J. and Krier, L., 'Classics Debate: Three Views on Modern Classics', *Architects' Journal*, 16th March 1988.

Street, G. E., *Account of Gothic Architecture in Spain* (London, 1865).

Summerson, Sir John, *Georgian London* (London, 1962).

Tallis, John, *London Street Views* (1838-39).

Swenarton, Mark, 'City of the Future', *Building Design*, 17th June 1988 [Describes Chicago's suburban downtowns].

Thackara, John, 'Design and the Age of Quality', *Design*, no. 412, April 1983.

Veblen, Thorstein, *The Theory of the Leisure Class* (1899).

Weber, Eugen, 'The Big Store', *Times Literary Supplement*, 13th November 1981.

Williams, Rosalind, *Dream Worlds: Mass Consumption in Late Nineteenth-Century France* (Berkeley, 1982).

Woudhuysen, James, 'Every Home a Videodrome', *Blueprint*, September 1988.

Zola, Emile, *Correspondence: VI 1887-1890* (Paris, 1987).

'The Designer and the Museum', *Metropolitan Museum of Art Bulletin*, no. 12, April 1917.

'The Industrial Art Exhibition', *Metropolitan Museum of Art Bulletin*, no. 19, February 1924.

'Enlivening a Variety of Objects: The Artist Creates Ideas for Industry', *Industrial Arts*, Autumn 1936.

'Design Centre', *Design*, no. 89, May 1956.

'Awards in Two Countries', *Design*, no. 150, June 1961.

California Environment (exh. cat., Los Angeles County Museum of Art, 1976).

Compasso d'oro 1954-1984 (exh. cat., Associazione Disegno Industriale, Milan, 1985).

Intellectual Property and Innovation (White Paper, 1986).

'Science and Technology: New York, Leonardo da IBM', *The Economist*, 27th August 1988.

Photographs were reproduced courtesy of the following:

André Malraux, Topham Picture Library; Walter Benjamin (Gisèle Freund), The John Hillelson Agency; Tom Wolfe (Jerry Bauer), Jonathan Cape Ltd; Emile Zola, Georges d'Avenel, Roger Viollet; Pierre Bourdieu, Polity Press; Vannevar Bush, The MIT Museum; 'Ace Caff', *Spectator*; Abbot Mead Vickers, 5; Architectural Association, 12, 18, 22, 62 (F. R. Yerbury), 100 (Dennis Crompton), 71 (B. Westwood); Ancient Art & Architecture Collection, 34, 46; *Architects' Journal* (Louis Helliman), 156; *Architecture from Prehistory to Post-Modernism*, Academy Editions, London, 1986, M. Irachtenburg & 1. Hyman, 93, 95, 96; AT&T Archives, a unit of the AT&T Library Network, 131; Benetton, 139-147; Benjamin Thompson & Associates, 114, 115, 116; Bernard Marrey, 66, 72, 73, 75; Boase Massimi Pollitt, 127; British Film Institute, 30, 45; Business Magazine (Dudley Reed), 118; Camera Press, 51; Chevejon, 74; Coca-Cola Company Great Britain Ltd, 122; The Conway Library / Courtauld Institute of Art, 28, 94; Design Analysis International, 135, 136, 137, 138; The Design Council, 112; Design Museum, 38, 42, 44, 52, 61, 63, 69, 70, 78, 81, 83, 84, 92 (Phil Sayer), 101, 102, 111, 117, 128, 130, 148, 149, 151, 150; English Heritage, 19; F. & C. Osler ltd, 59; Ferranti International, 132; Flaxyard P.l.c., 21, 26; Franca Helg, Architetti Associati, 113; Habitat Designs Ltd, 7; Imperial War Museum, 39; Keith Findlater, 61, 105; Kenwood Archive, 123; The Listener, 154, 155; Lloyd's of London, 106; Manchester City Central Reference Library, 87; Marcelle Johnbson, 13, 14; Markk Swenarton, 97, 98; Martin Charles, 20, 31, 32, 104; Mercury Communications, 23-25; The Trustees of Metropolitan Museum of Art, New York, 89, 90, 91; Milton Glaser, 54, 55, 56; Murjani, New York, 119; Museum of Classical Archaeology, Cambridge, 36; Museum of Modern Art, New York, 8, 109; Next P.l.c., 2, 4; Trustees of the National Gallery, London, 17; Olympia & York, 99, 107, 108; R.I.B.A., British Architectural Library, 15, 16, 43, 57, 103; Rowntree Mackintosh Confectionary Ltd, 126; Royal Commission on Historical Monuments, England, 33, 64, 65, 68; The Saatchi Collection, 9; Trustees of the Science Museum, London, 125; Staaliche Museen, Gemäldegalerie, Berlin (Schlöss Charlottenburg), 3; Stephen Parker, 35; Trustees of the Tate Gallery, London, 50, 67; Telefocus (British Telecom), 152; Topham Picture Library, 29; Toyota (UK) Ltd, 129; Tribune Media Services, 49; Victoria & Albert Museum, London, 11, 37, 40, 41, 80, 85, 86; Roger Viollet, 79; Washington, Hirshorn Museum, Smithsonian Institute, 48; WCRS Mathews Marcantonio, 6; Wedgwood Museum, Barlaston, 58, 60.

ACKNOWLEDGEMENTS

The Design Museum would like to thank the following for their help:

Artek

British Architectural Library

British Telecom

FIAT UK Ltd

Flaxyard plc

Franca Helg, Architetti Associati

Haslemere Estates

Holoscan

Society of Antiquaries, London (Kelmscott Manor)

Lord Reilly

Lutyens Design Associates

Manchester Polytechnic

Mercury Communications

Milton Glaser

Selfridge's Archive

Trustees of the Science Museum, London

Victoria & Albert Museum, London

Wedgwood Museum, Barlaston

Exhibitions Manager − Sarah Phillips

The Design Museum and David Davies Associates

would like to express special thanks to

Penshurst Press Limited

PENSHURST PRESS LIMITED

Buckingham House, Longfield Road, Tunbridge Wells, Kent TN2 3EY

Telephone: Tunbridge Wells (0892) 37315 Fax: (0892) 511424 Telex: 95414

Registered Number: 1352424 England